GRAIN
crazy

BRITNEY RULE AND CHERIE SCHETSELAAR

GRAIN *crazy*

RECIPES FOR

HEALTHY LIVING

familius

Published by Familius LLC, www.familius.com

Familius books are available at special discounts for bulk purchases for sales promotions, family or corporate use. Special editions, including personalized covers, excerpts of existing books, or books with corporate logos, can be created in large quantities for special needs. For more information, contact Premium Sales at 559-876-2170 or email specialmarkets@familius.com

Library of Congress Catalog-in-Publication Data
2013942877

pISBN: 978-1-938301-80-3
eISBN: 978-1-938301-81-0

Edited by Victoria Candland
Cover design by David Miles
Book design by Kurt Wahlner

10 9 8 7 6 5 4 3 2

First Edition

Contents

Grains 101   2

Breakfast   8

Quick Breads   26

Yeast Breads   44

Lunch   64

Snacks   82

Sides and Salads   94

Entrées   102

Desserts   120

Index   139

Grains 101

Grains have historically been the lifeblood of society. But in the last century, people have moved away from eating whole grains and moved to nutrient-empty white flour. As they have, obesity, high blood pressure, and heart disease have become almost epidemic conditions in the United States.

A whole-grain diet can greatly reduce these problems. Whole grains are rich in antioxidants, nutrients, and fiber. They have been shown to reduce the risk of heart disease and the likelihood of some types of cancer, including breast, colon, and kidney cancer. Whole grains can help regulate blood glucose, decreasing the risk of type 2 diabetes. They have even been shown to reduce risks of childhood asthma. And if that's not enough to convince you, people who regularly eat whole grains manage their weight on average better than those who don't.

The wonderful thing about grains is that they are easy to add to your family's daily diet–whether breakfasts, snacks, lunches, dinners, or desserts–in delicious and healthful ways.

In the past several years, my mother (Cherie) and I (Britney) have found great satisfaction in experimenting with whole grains in our cooking. In *Grain Crazy*, we've compiled our favorites. We hope you enjoy experimenting with whole grains in your cooking the way we have, and find the health benefits that they bring.

Whole Grains and Seeds

Whole grains have remarkable health benefits for your body. While grain is often made out to be the "bad guy" of our eating habits, it doesn't have to be. Whole grains have lots of nutrients, antioxidants, and health benefits. There are grains that are complete proteins, grains that have superpowers like lowering cholesterol, and grains that are remarkably gentle on your system.

A Whole Grain

A whole grain kernel is made up of three parts–the endosperm, the bran, and the germ. White flour is made up of only the endosperm. While the endosperm makes up the majority of the kernel, it contains very little of the fiber, protein, and vitamins. That is why white flour is usually enriched with other vitamins. The bran and germ, the parts that are removed, contain the majority of the fiber and nutrients. Wheat stripped of the bran and endosperm loses 25 percent of its protein and at least 17 nutrients.

When you buy foods, check to make sure that the first ingredient listed uses the word "whole." "Wheat flour" is simply not enough. You need "whole-wheat flour" or some other type of "whole-_____ flour." Many breads are colored darker to give the appearance of whole grains, or fiber may be added to give the nutrition facts the illusion of whole grain.

Getting Started

There are lots of ways to start using whole grains–and not all of them include bread products. Here are four of the easiest ways we've discovered to add whole grains to our cooking.

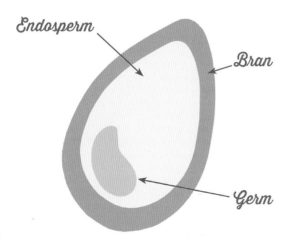

Endosperm

Bran

Germ

1. Adding Whole-Grain Flour to Your Baking
The most obvious way is to use a different kind of flour in your cooking. Spelt, Kamut®, brown rice, and oat flour are great choices to start with. Add half of one of these flours and half white flour to your recipes when you're just getting started, and then you can gradually add other combinations.

2. Use a Whole Grain Instead of White Rice

We love to add rice to a meal, but white rice adds almost no nutrition. Whip up a pilaf of brown rice, barley, quinoa, or millet, or a combination of them. These grains cook just like rice, but are much healthier.

3. Make a Whole-Grain Breakfast

Having oatmeal or multigrain breakfast cereal instead of store-bought cereal is a great start. Homemade granola or waffles, muffins, or pancakes with whole-grain flour are delicious.

4. Replace Your Snacks with Whole-Grain Alternatives

This substitution does take a little more planning, but it is worth it to avoid processed foods and sugars. Granola or popcorn can be a great snack, if you make it yourself.

5. Add Grain to a Soup

Soups can already be healthy meals, but adding a grain makes them more complete. Some good grains to add are barley, quinoa, and wheat berries.

Using Different Grains in Baking

Ideally you should use a mixture of grains in your cooking because they all offer different health benefits. Just as you should eat a variety of vegetables and fruits, the same holds true for grains.

One great flour mix for baking is 3 to 1 or 3 to 2 spelt to Kamut®. These grains are fairly easy to purchase, it's easier for a body to digest than other whole-grain flours, and it behaves similarly to wheat as it rises. The other benefit is that spelt and Kamut® are not genetically modified as heavily as wheat. Kamut® has no genetic modifications at all, and is always grown organically, which is an extra plus.

If you'd like to take it a step further, start by adding 1/2 cup of another flour of your choice to 3 cups of spelt. The flours you could add are nearly endless.

To lighten whole-grain yeast breads for a less dense product, you can add lecithin (add 2 tablespoons to your dough) or a store-bought dough enhancer. Use this in the beginning to help your family adjust, and then gradually adjust to a heavier finished product.

Different Grains

Here is an overview of different types of grains that we use in our cooking. While there are more grains than those listed, this will give you an understanding of the most common grains and what they are used for.

Whole Wheat

Whole-wheat flour, flour with the whole kernel of grain, is high in fiber, calcium, and potassium. Whole wheat may not be easy for everyone to digest, especially if they aren't used to it.

Uses: There are many different varieties of wheat, but there are three that you will find most frequently: soft white, hard white, and hard red. Soft white flour is lower in gluten, and is best used as a pastry flour in quick breads (breads that include baking powder or baking soda). Hard white is used in wheat breads, as it contains more gluten. Hard red wheat is the highest in protein, and will give you a heavier product than the other two.

Using whole-wheat flour instead of all-purpose flour will make your dough stickier. Do not add more flour, just lightly oil your hands to prevent it from sticking. Some people find that weighing their flour creates a more precise bread, as the flour can be more airy if it has just been ground.

Amaranth

Amaranth has a slightly nutty taste, is easily digestible, and has three times the fiber of

wheat. It's high in calcium, iron, and lysine and is totally gluten free. It has more protein than any other gluten-free grain, but is lower in carbs and contains polyunsaturated fatty acids.

Uses: Popped amaranth makes a delicious treat. You can also add amaranth flour to your flour mix. It cannot be used as an exclusive flour in most cooking because yeast breads won't raise well and pastry breads will be too heavy because of its high protein and fiber content. It is a great thickener for soups and sauces and is a lovely hot breakfast cereal.

 To pop amaranth, preheat a deep pot on medium high heat. Add no oil. Drop a pinch of amaranth into the pot. If it starts to pop, your temperature is correct. Cook about 2 to 3 tablespoons at a time. If you cook more than that at one time it will often burn. 1/4 cup of raw amaranth yields 1 cup of popped amaranth. Popped amaranth can be used in bread to give it a lighter texture. It is wonderful in cookies, breads, hot cereal, and salads.

Barley

Barley contains 8 essential amino acids and can help regulate blood sugar. A 1-cup serving has over 50 percent of your daily recommended fiber intake, and it is helpful in lowering cholesterol. It also has been attributed with preventing cardiovascular problems, lowering risk of heart failure, type 2 diabetes, and even childhood asthma.

Uses: Barley can be used in a pilaf or as a substitute for rice. It also works beautifully in soups and stews. You can substitute some of the flour in a recipe with barley flour to gain some of the health benefits, but don't use it exclusively because barley has a low gluten content.

Brown Rice

Brown rice is a quick and easy substitute for white rice that immediately turns a bowl full of carbs into a bowl full of nutrients. Like many grains, it's high in fiber, helps lower cholesterol, and can help lower cardiovascular disease. It is also full of manganese, an antioxidant that fights free radicals, and selenium, which helps regulate thyroid function and immune system functions. It also helps with bone health, as it contains magnesium. Brown rice is gluten-free.

Uses: Brown rice is a good side for any meal and combines well with many flavors. Rice flour can also be used in a flour mix, but don't use it alone–it will make a finished product that has drier, finer crumbs because it doesn't bind as well as a flour with gluten.

Buckwheat

Buckwheat is not really a grain, and it's not related to wheat. It's a fruit seed that's gluten-free and closer related to rhubarb and sorrel. But you can use it as if it were a grain, roasted or un-roasted (the roasted seed is also known as kasha), or as a flour. It's a good source of manganese, magnesium, and fiber, and it's a great protein, containing all eight essential amino acids.

Uses: You can grind buckwheat and use it in a flour mixture for baked goods, but we don't recommend using it alone. Add it to brown rice for a pilaf, boil it to make a breakfast cereal, or add it to soups and stews.

Chia

Do you remember Chia Pets? Same stuff. Chia is a healthy powerhouse. It has more omega 3s than salmon, 15 times more magnesium than broccoli, 3 times more iron than spinach, 6 times more calcium than milk, and 2 times more potassium than bananas. Also, 2 ounces of chia seeds gives you 560mg of vitamin C (almost 1,000 percent of your daily value). Chia is also great at aiding weight loss. Because it turns into a gel when you add water, it keeps you full longer. Chia does tend to be a little expensive, but you don't need a lot. Use it in tablespoons instead of cups.

Uses: Chia is virtually tasteless, and it doesn't take much to get the full nutritional benefit, so you can add it to breads, muffins, smoothies–virtually anything! Soak the seeds in water before you add them to food. Chia seeds absorb 10 times their own weight in water.

Flax

Flax is a little brown seed with plant-based omega-3 fatty acids, similar to those found in salmon. It can be beneficial in lowering cholesterol, blood triglyceride levels, and blood pressure. It's a great source of soluble and insoluble fiber, and it contains lignan, an antioxidant that has been shown to significantly reduce cancer, especially breast cancer.

Uses: Flax is easily added to lots of foods. Grind it for your body to absorb maximum nutrients. Sprinkle some on your cereal in the morning, on your salad, or in the dough you are baking, or add 1 tablespoon per serving into your smoothies. You don't need a lot to get the full health benefits.

 Do not put flax in your grinder!
Use a coffee grinder to break up the seeds to receive full nutritional benefits. Keep flax in the refrigerator or freezer to keep it fresh. This is a must if it is ground, otherwise the oils will start to spoil.

Kamut® (Khorasan Wheat)

The legend says that this grain was found in King Tut's tomb, but that is doubtful as its shelf life isn't that long. Kamut® looks a lot like wheat because it's a relative of durum wheat, but is larger, sweeter, healthier, and easier to digest than common wheat. It is rich in protein, selenium, zinc, and magnesium. It is often called a high-energy grain because it is especially rich in fatty acids. Kamut® is trademarked, ensuring that whenever you buy it, it is high quality, organically grown, and never genetically modified.

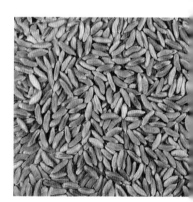

Uses: You can use Kamut® as a substitute for wheat in recipes, but be aware that it has less gluten than normal wheat. The berries, soaked overnight and then cooked on simmer for 45 minutes, are wonderful eaten like oatmeal, as a pilaf, or in salads and soups.

Millet

Millet is a grain that is especially gentle on the digestive system, so much so that some recommend using millet as Baby's first food instead of rice cereal. It is high in fiber and phosphorus and is gluten-free. It also contains the most complete protein of any other true cereal grain, and contains chemicals that lower cholesterol and reduce the risk of cancer.

Uses: Millet can also be used in pilafs as well as in a flour mixture for breads. Mix it with mashed potatoes to make them more nutritious. You can substitute it for white rice in any of your favorite recipes.

Since millet contains no gluten, it is not as good for raised bread by itself, although it will work in flatbread or when combined with wheat or xanthan gum.

Be careful digesting three or more servings of millet a day if you have hypothyroidism, as it can slow the intake of iodine to your body.

Oats

Oats are probably one of the most familiar whole grains, and they're wonderful for you! They contain more soluble fiber than any other grain, resulting in slower digestion and an extended sensation of fullness. They also contain beta-glucans, which have been proven to help lower LDL (bad) cholesterol, and therefore lower heart disease. They naturally contain no gluten, but are often grown alongside wheat and barley. Oats are only okay for people with Celiac Disease to eat if they are certified gluten free.

Oats typically are sold in a variety of processed forms. Starting with the least processed and moving to more processed, you can find:

1. Oat groats: whole kernel with the tough hull removed, retaining the bran and the germ of the grain

2. Steel-cut oats: groats cut into smaller pieces

3. Rolled oats: steel-cut oats that have been flattened

4. Quick cooking or instant: further processed oats, retaining less of the nutrients than the other versions

5. Oat bran: Just the bran part of the oat kernel

6. Oat flour: Oat groats ground into flour

Uses: You are already familiar with eating rolled oats in porridge form, as granola, or as an ingredient in cookies. We use it frequently as a flour in both yeast and quick breads. Any form of oats, from groats to rolled oats, are great for porridge, but the less they are processed, the longer they need to cook.

Quinoa

Pronounced "keen-wa," quinoa is a supergrain that comes from the Andes of South America, and was one of the Mayan civilization's staple foods. It not only contains more protein than any other grain, but it is also a complete protein, meaning it contains all eight essential amino acids, just like milk. It is light, easy to digest, and high in lysine.

Uses: A great way to use quinoa is as a substitute for rice. Quinoa makes an excellent pilaf or salad, and cooks the same way white rice is cooked. Quinoa can also be ground like wheat and used in baking, though it is usually used in a multi-grain mixture instead of on its own.

Rye

Rye is an excellent source of manganese, containing over 75 percent of your recommended daily value in a serving. It has a lot of fiber that keeps you feeling satiated. It has a deep, rich, hearty flavor, and although it is low in gluten, it is not gluten-free.

Uses: Rye is usually used as a flour, but can also be eaten in its berry form in breakfast cereals or salads. In breads, it is usually used as one third of the total amount of flour.

Spelt

Spelt is a member of the wheat family that is still eaten regularly in Europe. It has not been used as often in America, but because of that, it has not been heavily genetically modified. Spelt looks similar to wheat, but has a harder outer shell, and many people describe the taste as nutty and slightly sweet. It is easier to digest than whole wheat, and has less gluten that breaks down easily, making it preferable to people with wheat sensitivities. It has slightly less fiber than wheat, but more protein and fewer calories.

Uses: Spelt is a great substitute for white flour in baking. Because the gluten breaks down more easily than in whole-wheat flour, dough doesn't need as much kneading as whole-wheat flour to activate the gluten, and may not rise as high. It often needs a bit less liquid because it's more water soluble.

Teff

Teff is a grain that is common in Ethiopia, coming in a variety of colors. The most common is brown. The grains of teff are very small (it takes about 150 teff grains to weigh the same as 1 wheat kernel), which means it needs less fuel to cook, making it an important food source for those living in the desert.

Because the grain is so small, most of the grain consists of the bran and germ portions of the kernel, meaning it is packed with nutrients. Teff is very high in calcium (more than milk), and contains all eight essential amino acids necessary for humans. It is gluten-free, and high in protein, fiber, and many other essential minerals.

Uses: Teff is fantastic as flour. It works great as a substitute for part of the wheat flour in breads. It works especially well for quick breads such as pancakes and muffins. It tastes great in stews, pilaf, or porridge. Since it is so small, it also can be served whole as a substitute for seeds, such as sesame seeds.

Other Grains to Try

Frika or Gruenkern: green (unripe) spelt with a smoky flavor

Farro: an Italian strain of wheat

Polenta and Grits: both ground cornmeal, though method and fineness of each are different

Red Quinoa

Sorghum

Triticale

Legume flours

Coconut flour

Corn

Popcorn

Durham Wheat

Couscous

Breakfast

Spelt Pancakes

We are picky about pancakes. They must be light and moist. These pancakes meet our requirements nicely and can be made quickly.

2 cups of spelt flour	2 tablespoons of coconut oil
2 teaspoons of baking powder	1 tablespoon of honey
$1/4$ teaspoon of salt	1 $1/2$ cups of almond milk, unsweetened
1 teaspoon of cinnamon	Your favorite topping
2 eggs, beaten	

1. Heat a greased griddle to around 300 degrees.

2. Mix all the dry ingredients in a bowl with a wire whisk.

3. Add eggs, oil, honey, and milk. Stir until just mixed.

4. Pour the batter on griddle in 4-inch pancakes. Cook until lightly golden on both sides. Top with your favorite topping.

Serves 8

Spelt Waffles

Fresh or frozen strawberries work great to give these waffles a little natural sweetener.

2 cups of spelt flour or whole-grain flour

2 tablespoons of cornmeal

1 teaspoon of salt

$^{1}/_{2}$ teaspoon of baking soda

2 large eggs

$^{1}/_{4}$ cup of coconut oil, melted

1 $^{3}/_{4}$ cups of kefir, plain yogurt, or buttermilk

$^{1}/_{4}$ cup water

2 tablespoons of honey

1 teaspoon of lemon juice (optional)

1 teaspoon of lemon zest (optional)

2 teaspoons of cream of tartar

1. In a medium-sized bowl, mix flour, cornmeal, salt, and baking soda with a wire whisk. Set aside.

2. Separate the eggs in two separate bowls, one for the yolks and one for the whites. Into the bowl containing the egg yolks, stir in the oil, kefir, honey, lemon juice, and zest. Stir the egg yolk mixture into the flour mixture.

3. Beat the egg whites and cream of tartar until stiff peaks form. Gently fold into the flour mixture. Set aside for 5 to 10 minutes to let the batter rise.

4. Bake the waffles in a preheated waffle iron.

5. Serve warm with your favorite syrup and berries or bananas.

Makes 8 waffles

Spelt

Anciently, spelt was cultivated as commonly as wheat or corn are cultivated today. Though now mostly considered a health food, spelt is becoming more popular around the world.

Grind it Out

Our flour mixture includes 4 cups of spelt, 2 cups of Kamut®, 1 cup of brown rice, 1 cup of buckwheat, and 1 cup of oat groats. We grind a large amount and put the extra flour mixture into the refrigerator until we need it again.

Tasty Buttermilk Blueberry Pancakes

Mom's kids at home enjoy pancakes any morning!

2 eggs	1 ½ teaspoons of coconut oil
1 cup of buttermilk	2 teaspoons of baking powder
2 teaspoons of vanilla	1 ½ to 2 cups of whole-grain flour
1 tablespoon of honey	Fresh blueberries

1. Heat a greased griddle to around 300 degrees.

2. In a large bowl, beat the eggs, buttermilk, vanilla, honey, and oil. Set aside.

3. In a separate bowl, add the flour and baking powder and whisk together. Slowly stir the flower mixture into the milk mixture. Do not over stir. Start with 1 ½ cups of flour and add more as needed. You don't want the batter too thick.

4. Pour the batter on griddle in 4-inch pancakes. Cook until lightly golden on both sides. Top with your favorite topping.

Makes about 10 pancakes

 Tip:

If you don't have buttermilk, add 1 tablespoon of vinegar to 1 cup of milk and let it sit for 5 minutes. Kefir can also be used in place of butter-milk.

Baked Oatmeal

The great thing about this recipe is that it can be made ahead and stored.

2 cups of old-fashioned oatmeal

$^1/_4$ cup of flax seeds, ground

1 teaspoon of baking powder

1 teaspoon of cinnamon

$^1/_2$ teaspoon of ginger

$^1/_2$ teaspoon of nutmeg

$^1/_4$ teaspoon of ground cloves

$^1/_4$ teaspoon of cardamom (optional)

$^1/_2$ teaspoon of salt

2 $^1/_2$ cups of milk

$^1/_4$ to $^1/_3$ cup of honey

1 egg

$^1/_4$ cup of coconut oil, melted

1 teaspoon of vanilla

$^1/_2$ cup of dried fruit or nuts (optional)

1. Preheat oven to 350 degrees. Grease 8 ramekins or a 2-quart baking dish.

2. In a large bowl, mix together oats, flax seeds, baking powder, spices, and salt.

3. In a different bowl, mix milk, honey, egg, coconut oil, and vanilla until all combined.

4. Mix the wet and dry ingredients together. Fold in the fruit and nuts if desired. For a softer mixture, let it sit in the refrigerator overnight.

5. Pour into greased ramekins or 2-quart baking dish. Bake 25 to 35 minutes. It should turn a nice golden brown. Serve warm with milk and fresh fruit.

Serves 8

Chocolate Almond Butter Oatmeal

We love chocolate and almond flavors together. We find the 6-grain rolled oat mixture at our local health foods store. You can substitute 6-grain oats with old-fashioned oats.

2 cups of water

2 cups of almond milk

1 tablespoon of coconut oil

2 cups of 6-grain rolled oats

3 tablespoons of unsweetened cocoa

3 tablespoons of almond butter or peanut butter

2 to 3 tablespoons of honey

1 teaspoon of almond extract

Top with milk, fresh bananas, fresh fruit, or chocolate chips

1. Boil water in a medium saucepan. Add milk and oil. Stir in oatmeal. Bring mixture to a low boil.

2. Stir in cocoa, almond butter, honey, and almond extract. Reduce heat to low. Cook until the mixture thickens and reaches your desired consistency.

3. Serve in bowls and put on your favorite topping.

Serves 5 to 6

Other Topping Ideas

Chocolate chips or fresh apple slices also make this oatmeal a special treat. Alternately, stir in pumpkin puree or peanut butter. There are lots of possibilities!

Cinnanut Oatmeal

You always win with the combination of oatmeal and cinnamon. This breakfast is a great way to start your day. The nuts can also be used in other hot cereals.

4 tablespoons of coconut sugar or brown sugar

4 tablespoons of water

$1/2$ teaspoon of butter

$1/2$ teaspoon of cinnamon

1 pinch of salt

$1/2$ cup of walnuts or other nuts, finely chopped

4 cups of water

2 cups of old-fashioned oatmeal

1 tablespoon of coconut oil

1 pinch of salt

1 tablespoon of coconut sugar

Top with bananas, berries, fruit, sugar, or milk if desired

1. In a small saucepan heat the sugar, butter, cinnamon, salt, and 4 tablespoons of water until just before boiling. Stir in the nuts. Bring to a boil and cook while stirring until the mixture thickens. Pour onto parchment paper or waxed paper to cool.

2. Boil 4 cups of water in a medium-sized pot. Stir in oats, oil, salt, and sugar. Bring to a boil again, then reduce the heat and cover for 10 minutes. Longer cooking will result in softer oatmeal.

3. Serve with the nut mixture on top.

Serves 8

Gluten Free?

Pure oats are gluten free, but because they are often processed in facilities that work with other grains, there's always a chance the normal oats at the store could be unsafe. To enjoy gluten-free oatmeal, use certified gluten-free oats.

Creamy Spelt Berry Oatmeal

This hearty, hot cereal tastes so good. It's loaded with a lot of great whole grains. It is a wonderful way to start your day because it's satisfying and healthy. (Instructions on how to cook spelt berries can be found on page 81.)

2 cups of milk

1 1/4 cups of old-fashioned oatmeal

3 tablespoons of ground flax (optional)

1 to 2 tablespoons of coconut oil (adds a creamy texture)

1/2 cup of raisins

1 1/4 cups of spelt berries (You can also use wheat or Kamut®.)

2 to 3 tablespoons of honey

1 teaspoon of cinnamon

1/2 teaspoon of freshly grated ginger (optional)

Top with freshly grated nutmeg, unsweetened coconut, dried cranberries, or chopped nuts

1. In a saucepan, slowly bring the milk to a boil, careful not to scald. Stir in oats, flax, oil, and raisins. Reduce heat to low and cover. Let simmer for 3 minutes.

2. Stir in cooked spelt berries, honey, and spices. Cook until completely warm.

3. Top with your favorite topping. A little milk on top is delicious!

Serves 4

Amaranth and Quinoa Hot Cereal

Tart apples are the perfect combination with this breakfast cereal, and the amaranth is loaded with lots of nutrition. Try it for lunch sometime—it's a nice change from the usual sandwich.

3 tablespoons of quinoa	$1/3$ cup of milk of your choice
3 tablespoons of amaranth	$1/2$ teaspoon of cinnamon
1 cup of water	$1/4$ teaspoon of fresh nutmeg
1 tablespoon of coconut oil	Top with fruit and unsweetened coconut, or even diced Granny Smith apples
1 tablespoon of honey	

1. Lightly toast the quinoa and amaranth in a saucepan for 3 to 5 minutes. You should smell a nice aroma. Be careful not to let it burn. Carefully add the water and bring to a boil. Add the coconut oil. Reduce heat to low, cover, and simmer for 30 minutes.

2. Uncover and stir in the milk and spices. Simmer another 3 to 5 minutes.

3. Serve topped with coconut, fruit, and more milk if desired.

Serves 2

Amaranth

Amaranth was a major source of calories for the ancient Aztecs. Today, amaranth is known for its high fiber and protein, and is delicious when popped!

Quinoa and Teff Hot Cereal

This hot cereal utilizes some grains that, unfortunately, are seldom used.

1 cup of quinoa

1/2 cup of teff

2 tablespoons of coconut oil

2 cups of milk

1/2 cup of water

1 to 2 tablespoons of honey

1/2 teaspoon of cinnamon

1/4 teaspoon of nutmeg

Top with currants, raisins, or other fruit

1. Rinse the quinoa in a strainer. Lightly toast the quinoa and teff in a saucepan.

2. Stir in oil, milk, water, honey, cinnamon, and nutmeg. Bring to a boil. Cover and reduce heat to low. Cook for about 20 minutes, or until the liquid is absorbed and the grains are soft.

3. Serve with fruit and a little milk if desired. Yum!

Serves 4

Millet Cranberry Cereal

This is a healthier version of Rice Krispies Treats® cereal. Use unsweetened cranberries and freshly ground almond butter for an especially fresh dish.

1 cup of almond butter or creamy peanut butter

$^2/_3$ cup of honey

2 teaspoons of vanilla

2 cups of old-fashioned oatmeal

3 cups of puffed millet

$^1/_2$ cup of dried cranberries or different dried fruit

1 teaspoon of cinnamon

1. In a saucepan, slowly heat the butter and honey until the mixture reaches a smooth consistency. Remove from heat and stir in vanilla.

2. In a separate bowl, mix the oatmeal and millet together with the cinnamon and cranberries. Pour in hot mixture and mix together.

3. Grease a 13x9-inch pan. Pour the mixture into the pan and flatten. You can use plastic wrap or waxed paper to keep your hands clean. After it's hardened slightly, break the cereal into pieces and store in a zipper-topped bag.

4. Serve it in bowls with milk.

Serves 8

Quick Breads

Pear Ginger Muffins

Pears make an unconventional but wonderful addition to muffins. They taste similar to apples, but are slightly sweeter. Try them with fresh ginger.

2 cups of Kamut® flour (or another whole grain)

2 cups of old-fashioned oatmeal

5 tablespoons of honey or 6 tablespoons of packed brown sugar

1 tablespoon of baking powder

1 teaspoon of ground ginger or 1 ½ teaspoons of freshly grated ginger

1 teaspoon of cinnamon

½ teaspoon of fresh nutmeg

½ teaspoon of salt

1 ⅓ cups of milk or kefir or yogurt

½ cup of water

½ cup of coconut oil, melted, or ⅔ cup of another oil

2 eggs

1 ½ cups of pears, chopped in small pieces

½ cup of nuts almonds, walnuts, or pecans, chopped

1. Preheat oven to 400 degrees. Grease muffin tins.

2. Measure all dry ingredients in a large bowl. Stir with a wire whisk.

3. In a smaller bowl, beat milk, water, oil, and eggs until combined.

4. Make a well in the dry ingredients and pour in the liquid mixture. Stir with the wire whisk until just combined.

5. Fold in the pears and nuts, if desired.

6. Scoop the batter into the greased muffin tins. Bake for 15 to 18 minutes, or until muffins are lightly golden.

7. Let the muffins cool for 5 minutes and then turn them out on wire cooling racks.

Makes 24 muffins

An Ode to the Blueberry

Blueberries are a wonderful fruit we can enjoy all year-round thanks to the freezer. Here are some of the benefits in an abbreviated form. No wonder they are called a super food. Blueberries:

1. are good for brain health.

2. reduce heart disease.

3. help aid digestion.

4. may reduce some forms of cancers.

5. help to preserve vision.

6. can be an anti-depressant.

7. aid in reducing belly fat.

8. have the highest antioxidant capacity of all fresh fruits.

Banana Blueberry Muffins

When we make muffins and other baked goods, we reduce the sweetener and we add more spices. The spices add an extra boost to the flavor.

2 ripe bananas, mashed

1 ¹/₂ cups of kefir or plain yogurt

¹/₂ cup of honey

²/₃ cup of olive oil

4 teaspoons of vanilla

5 cups of whole-grain flour

4 teaspoons of baking powder

2 teaspoons of cinnamon, heaping

1 teaspoon of baking soda

1 teaspoon of salt

2 cups of blueberries

1. Preheat oven to 425 degrees. Grease muffin tins.

2. Mix the banana, kefir, honey, oil, and vanilla together.

3. In a separate bowl, mix all the dry ingredients together. Combine the dry ingredients with the wet ingredients. Gently fold in the blueberries.

4. Scoop the mixture into the greased muffin tins. Bake for 8 to 9 minutes.

Makes 24 muffins

🌾 *Tip:*

We use a flour mixture of equal parts oat, Kamut®, and spelt flour.

Peach Pie Muffins

We can't get enough peaches when they are in season. While Mom's favorite way to eat them is with vanilla ice cream, this recipe is more appropriate for a morning gathering with friends.

1 1/2 cups of whole-grain flour

1 1/2 teaspoons of baking powder

1/2 teaspoon of salt

1 teaspoon of cinnamon

1/2 teaspoon of cardamom

1/2 teaspoon of fresh nutmeg or 1/4 teaspoon of dried nutmeg

2 cups of old-fashioned oatmeal

1 1/2 cups of milk

2 eggs, beaten

1/3 cup of coconut oil

1/2 cup honey

2 ripe peaches, diced

1. Preheat oven to 400 degrees. Grease muffin tins.

2. Mix the flour, baking powder, salt, cinnamon, cardamom, and nutmeg together.

3. In a separate bowl, mix the oatmeal and milk together to soften the oatmeal. Set aside for 5 to 10 minutes.

4. Mix the oatmeal mixture with the beaten eggs, oil, and honey.

 Tip:

We use 1/2 cup of Kamut®, 3/4 cup of spelt, and 1/4 cup of teff flour.

5. Fold the oatmeal mixture into the flour mixture.

6. Fold in the diced peaches.

7. Pour the mixture into the greased muffin tins. Bake for 15 to 20 minutes. Remove them from the pan, dust them with powdered sugar, and enjoy!

Makes about 38 mini muffins

Carrot Orange Spice Muffins

Whole-grain muffins can be a little heavy, but these muffins are light. Did you know that the greens of the carrots are also edible? Humans rarely eat them, though.

3 cups of whole-grain flour

4 teaspoons of baking powder

1 teaspoon of baking soda

1 $\frac{1}{2}$ teaspoons of cinnamon

1 teaspoon of fresh grated ginger or 2 teaspoons of ground ginger

$\frac{1}{2}$ cup of coconut oil

$\frac{1}{3}$ cup of honey

2 eggs

$\frac{2}{3}$ cup of milk

4 tablespoons of orange juice, unsweetened

2 teaspoons of orange zest

2 teaspoons of vanilla

$\frac{1}{2}$ cup of unsweetened shredded coconut (optional)

2 cups of grated carrots

1. Preheat oven to 375 degrees. Grease a mini muffin tin.

2. In a medium bowl, combine the flour, baking powder, baking soda, cinnamon, and ginger.

3. In a separate bowl, cream the oil, honey, and eggs. Add the milk, juice, zest, and vanilla. Stir in the carrots. Stir the dry ingredients into the wet mixture. Don't over stir.

4. Scoop the combined mixture into the greased mini muffin tin and bake for 10 to 12 minutes, or until the muffins are golden. Cooking time will depend on muffin size.

Makes 35 mini muffins

 *Tip:*

We grind up 3 cups of spelt, 2 cups of Kamut®, 1 cup of buckwheat, 1 cup of brown rice, and 1 cup of oat groats for this recipe's flour. There is sometimes extra flour left over to use in other cooking.

Strawberry Banana Muffins

These muffins contain five different grains. They are healthy and taste good at the same time.

4 overripe bananas, mashed	4 $^1/_2$ cups of whole-grain flour
3 large eggs	3 teaspoons of baking powder
$^2/_3$ cup of honey	1 teaspoon of salt
$^1/_2$ cup of coconut oil	$^1/_2$ teaspoon of baking soda
2 teaspoons of vanilla	2 cups of strawberries, diced
$^1/_2$ cup of plain yogurt	

 *Tip:*

We grind 2 cups of spelt, 1 cup of Kamut®, $^1/_4$ cup of buckwheat, $^1/_4$ cup of amaranth, $^1/_4$ cup of brown rice. There is usually a small amount left over.

1. Preheat oven to 350 degrees. Grease muffin tins.

2. Place the peeled bananas in a glass bowl. Cover the bowl with plastic and microwave on high for about 5 minutes. Strain out the liquid (which should be about $^1/_2$ cup). Pour the liquid into a saucepan and boil until reduced to $^1/_4$ cup. Set it aside to cool.

3. In a medium-sized bowl, beat the eggs, honey, oil, vanilla, yogurt, mashed bananas, and liquid from bananas with a wire whisk. Set the mixture aside.

4. In a separate bowl, whisk the flour, baking powder, soda, salt, and cinnamon. Gently fold in the strawberries until they are completely covered with flour.

5. Fold in the wet ingredients. The batter should be lumpy.

6. Scoop the mixture into the greased muffin tin.

7. Bake the muffins for 10 to 12 minutes, or until they are barely golden.

Makes 46 mini muffins

🌾 Tip:

Use a cookie scooper to make all your muffins the same size.

Pumpkin Bread

During the autumn, Mom starts craving all things pumpkin. We see a lot of pumpkin at that time of year. This recipe satisfies with four different whole grains.

$^3/_4$ cup of Kamut® flour

$^3/_4$ cup of spelt flour

1 cup of oat flour

1 cup of quinoa flour

1 tablespoon and 1 teaspoon of cinnamon

1 teaspoon of baking soda

2 teaspoons of baking powder

2 teaspoons of pumpkin spice

$^1/_2$ teaspoon of fresh nutmeg or 1 teaspoon of ground nutmeg

2 eggs

1 cup of honey

1 $^1/_2$ cups of plain honey

1 $^1/_2$ cups of canned pumpkin

6 tablespoons of coconut oil or another oil

1 tablespoon of vanilla

1. Preheat oven to 350 degrees. Grease loaf pans.

2. Whisk all the dry ingredients in a medium-sized bowl.

3. In a separate bowl, beat the eggs, honey, yogurt, pumpkin, oil, and vanilla.

4. Fold the dry ingredients into the wet ingredients. Stir until combined.

5. Pour the mixture into the greased loaf pans and bake for 30 to 40 minutes.

Makes 3 small or 2 medium-sized loaves.

Pumpkin

According to the United States Department of Agriculture, the United States produces over one billion pounds of pumpkin every year. That's a whole lot of pumpkin bread!

Old Fashioned Oatmeal Bars

This moist cake could take the place of a morning bowl of oatmeal, and the addition of an apple makes it one step closer to a complete meal. You can also add nuts or fruit.

1 $1\frac{1}{2}$ cups of boiling water

1 cup of oatmeal

$\frac{1}{3}$ cup of coconut oil

$\frac{2}{3}$ cup of honey

2 large eggs

$1\frac{1}{2}$ cups of whole-grain flour

$\frac{1}{4}$ teaspoon of salt

1 teaspoon of vanilla

1 teaspoon of baking soda

1 teaspoon of cinnamon

$\frac{1}{4}$ cup of shredded coconut

1 small apple, grated

Tip:

We use 1 cup of spelt and $\frac{1}{2}$ cup of Kamut® flours.

1. Preheat over to 325 degrees. Grease a 9x13-inch pan.

2. In a saucepan, boil water. Remove from heat and pour in the oatmeal. Let sit for 15 minutes.

3. Cream the oil, honey, and eggs together. Add cooked oatmeal, flour, salt, vanilla, soda, cinnamon, coconut, and apple and mix, being careful not to overmix.

4. Pour the mixture into the greased 9x13-inch pan and bake for 20 to 25 minutes.

Serves 12

Chocolate Zucchini Muffins

These are wonderfully moist muffins. They have the perfect combination of chocolate and zucchini and these muffins are good for you!

1 egg

³/₄ cup of unsweetened applesauce

¹/₂ cup of honey

¹/₃ cup of almond milk

2 tablespoons of coconut oil

1 teaspoon of vanilla extract

1 ¹/₄ cups of zucchini, grated

2 cups of whole-grain flour (I use 1 cup of Kamut® and 1 cup of spelt)

1 teaspoon of baking powder

³/₄ teaspoon of baking soda

¹/₂ teaspoon of salt

1 teaspoon of cinnamon

¹/₂ cup of dark chocolate chips (optional)

5. Heat the oven to 350 degrees. Grease the mini muffin tin. Mix the egg, applesauce, honey, milk, oil, vanilla, and zucchini until combined. Set the mixture aside.

6. In another bowl, whisk together the flour, baking powder, soda, salt, and cinnamon. Fold into the wet mixture until combined. If desired, fold in chocolate chips.

7. Scoop batter into the muffin tins and bake for 10 to 15 minutes.

Makes about 24 mini muffins

Tips to Improve Your Muffins

1. Don't ever beat them with a mixer. Fold the ingredients together instead. The batter should be lumpy.

2. Beat the wet ingredients in a separate bowl before adding it to the dry ingredients.

3. Using a cookie scoop works great for scooping the batter into the muffin tins.

4. Remove muffins from the pan quickly after taking them out of the oven. If left in the pan they will continue to cook and dry out.

5. If you are adding frozen berries to your muffins, do not thaw them before adding. They will be mushy.

Muffin Cook Time

We often make mini muffins, but you can adjust these recipes for any size of muffin. To make standard sized muffins from a recipe that makes mini muffins, add 5 to 8 minutes of baking time. Add 15 to 20 minutes to make jumbo muffins. If the recipe is already making standard-sized muffins, take off 5 to 8 minutes to make mini muffins or add 8 to 13 minutes to make jumbo muffins. There are about 3 mini muffins in a standard muffin.

Yeast Breads

Whole-Grain Rolls

Rolls are often the best part of a meal! Switch out white rolls for this easy whole-grain version.

4 cups of warm water	1 teaspoon of salt
2 tablespoons of yeast	2 tablespoons of gluten
$^2/_3$ cup of honey	3 cups of whole-wheat flour
$^1/_3$ cup of coconut oil or another oil	4 cups of spelt flour
$^1/_3$ cup of nonfat powdered milk	4 cups of Kamut®, amaranth, oat, flour
1 egg	$^1/_2$ cup of sunflower seeds (optional)

1. In a bowl, combine the water, yeast, and honey. Let it sit until it starts to bubble–about 5 or 10 minutes. Add the oil, milk, egg, salt, and gluten. Beat together.

2. Add the flour a little bit at a time. You want to add enough flour so the dough is still sticky to the touch. It should not be as dry as bread dough. Knead the dough for 5 minutes. Cover and let rise for 20 to 30 minutes.

3. Preheat oven to 350 degrees.

4. Form the dough into rolls the size of your own choosing. Gently press the tops of the rolls into a bowl of sunflower seeds, if desired. Place the rolls on a baking sheet. Let them rise until they are double in size.

5. Bake the rolls for 10 to 12 minutes or until golden.

6. We like to rub butter over the top and serve with butter and jam!

Makes 24 rolls

 Tip:

We grind $^1/_4$ cup of amaranth, 1 $^1/_2$ cup of oats, and 1 $^1/_2$ cup of Kamut® for flour.

Whole-Grain Cinnamon Roll Bread

One of our favorite kinds of bread is cinnamon bread. Store bought is expensive and not very healthy, so we created our own whole-grain pull-apart bread. It is easy to make and gets gobbled up fast. It is a great way to get your family to eat whole-grain bread.

3 cups of hot water	1 $\frac{1}{2}$ tablespoons of yeast
$\frac{1}{3}$ cup of honey	7 to 8 cups of whole-grain flour
1 $\frac{1}{4}$ teaspoons of salt with iodine	Butter
$\frac{1}{3}$ cup of coconut oil	Cinnamon
2 tablespoons of lecithin granules	Brown sugar
1 tablespoon of plain yogurt	

1. Preheat oven to 350 degrees. Grease 2 9-inch loaf pans

2. Combine water, honey, salt, oil, lecithin, and yogurt. Blend together in a bread mixer or by hand.

3. Add 2 cups of flour and knead for 2 to 3 minutes. Add the yeast.

4. Knead the dough and add the flour one cup at a time until the dough no longer sticks to the sides of the bowl. Knead for 10 minutes. Then let it rest for 5 to 10 minutes.

5. Divide the dough into 2 sections.

6. Roll out the first section in a rectangle shape about $1/4$ inch thick. Brush on a thin layer of butter and then dust with a small amount of brown sugar and cinnamon. Roll up tight. Cut the roll into $3/4$-inch pieces with a serrated knife. Repeat with the second section.

7. Place the cinnamon rolls close together on their sides in the greased loaf pans. Cover with a towel and let rise until double in size.

8. Bake for 20 minutes. Make sure the rolls cook all the way through. Brush butter on top when out of the oven. Cool briefly on a cooling rack. Serve warm.

Makes 2 9-inch loaves

 Tip:

We grind 2 $1/2$ cups of white wheat, 1 $1/2$ cup of spelt, 1 cup of buckwheat, and 1 cup of oatmeal for this recipe. You can also use whole wheat.

Whole-Grain Hamburger Buns

Next time you are in the store, look at the list of ingredients in the hamburger buns, and then make your own instead. Try them with our Homemade Hamburgers on page 104.

1 ½ cups of warm water	3 eggs
1 ⅓ tablespoons of yeast	2 teaspoons of salt
5 tablespoons of honey	4 to 5 cups of whole-grain flour
6 tablespoons of olive oil	1 cup of white flour

 Tip:

I use 3 cups of spelt flour, 1 cup of Kamut® flour, 1 cup of oat flour, and 1 cup of white flour. You could use whole-wheat flour, or ½ wheat and white flour.

1. Preheat oven to 375 degrees. Grease a cookie sheet.

2. In a bread mixer or bowl, add water, yeast, and honey. Let the mixture stand in the bowl for 5 to 10 minutes to rise.

3. Add oil, eggs, salt, and 3 cups of flour and mix. Slowly add more flour until the dough pulls away from the bowl as it's mixed. Knead for 3 to 5 minutes; the dough should still be sticky. Allow the dough to rest for 10 minutes.

4. Oil your hands and roll the dough into balls. Place the balls on the greased cookie sheet. Let them rise until they are double in size.

5. Bake for 12 to 15 minutes or until a light golden color. Rub butter on top of the rolls, if desired.

6. Place the rolls on a cooling rack to avoid over baking.

7. Slice and serve with your favorite hamburger recipe.

Makes 12 buns

Indian Flatbread

This is a fun flat bread to try. Serve it with your favorite Indian dish.

2 cups of whole-wheat flour	1 tablespoon of olive oil
1 $\frac{1}{2}$ teaspoons of salt	1 tablespoon of oil for frying, if desired
$\frac{3}{4}$ cup of water	Butter or coconut oil (optional)

1. In a bowl, sift the flour and salt together.

2. Stir in the water and mix until it becomes a soft dough. Knead in the oil.

3. Place the dough on a smooth surface. Oil your hands and knead the dough for about 5 minutes.

4. Place the dough in a bowl with a small amount of oil and turn the dough so it is covered with oil. Cover and let stand for 30 minutes.

5. Divide the dough into 6 to 8 round balls. Place each ball into the palm of your hand one at a time. Press between your hands until you form flat circles. Cover with plastic while you prepare the other balls.

6. Heat a griddle or heavy frying pan on medium heat. You can pour in 1 tablespoon of oil if desired.

7. Fry 60 seconds on the first side, or until it starts to bubble. Turn over and fry on the other side for another 30 seconds.

8. Place flatbread between dishtowels to keep warm while you cook the remaining balls.

9. After frying, brush the flatbread with butter or oil if desired. Serve while warm.

Makes 6 to 8 pieces of flatbread

Pita Bread

This recipe is a way to enjoy pita bread with some whole grain added.

2 ¼ cups of wheat flour	2 tablespoons of olive oil
2 tablespoons of yeast	1 cup of warm water (about 110 degrees)
1 tablespoon of salt	2 cups of white flour

1. Dissolve the yeast in water. Combine with all other ingredients. Knead until soft and not too sticky.

2. Place the dough in an oiled bowl. Cover with a towel and let rise for at least 30 minutes (or up to 2 hours).

3. Knead the dough again for 10 minutes, or until it is smooth.

4. Place the dough back into the oiled bowl. Cover and place in a warm area until the dough is doubled in size.

5. Divide the dough into 12 balls of equal size, about ½ inch in diameter.

6. With a rolling pin, roll the balls flat. Keep the flattened balls covered as you roll out the others so they don't dry out.

7. Heat a frying pan on medium-high heat. Cook each pita on one side for about 20 seconds. Flip and cook for 1 minute more.

8. Serve hot.

Makes 12 pitas

Oatmeal Honey Spelt Bread

This bread reminds us of bread at restaurants. It is fun to find a whole-grain bread that has the same flavor. We are guessing the breads at restaurants are not all whole grains. It's just a hunch!

1 1/2 cups of old-fashioned oatmeal

2 tablespoons of butter or coconut oil

1 1/2 cups of water boiling water

1/3 cup of honey

1 tablespoon of salt

1 1/2 cups of warm water (about 110 degrees)

3 1/2 teaspoons of yeast

6 1/2 to 7 cups of whole-grain flour

1 1/2 cups of rolled oatmeal

1. Preheat over to 400 degrees. Grease 2 9-inch bread pans.

2. In a metal bowl, pour in the oatmeal and butter. Then pour 1 1/2 cups boiling water over both. Stir until mixed. Put aside and let cool to room temperature. You can start the soaking process the night before and let sit overnight to increase the nutritional benefits.

3. Pour in all of the other ingredients in a bread mixer or bowl, except the additional oatmeal. Knead, adding 1 cup of flour at a time until the dough pulls away from the sides of the bowl. Don't let it get too dry. The dough should still be sticky.

 Tip:

I used 3 1/2 cups of wheat flour and 3 1/2 cups of spelt flour.

4. Knead for 3 to 4 minutes. Let the dough rest for 10 minutes. Knead for 2 more minutes.

5. Place dough in slightly oiled bowl that is double the size of the dough. Cover the dough with plastic wrap and let it rise until double. Deflate the dough and let it double one more time.

6. Punch down the dough. Divide the dough in half and roll each half into a loaf. Pour $3/4$ cup of the oatmeal on a rectangle piece of parchment paper and spread. Roll the loaf on the oatmeal until the top and sides are covered. Repeat the process with the second loaf.

7. Place each loaf in a greased 9-inch bread pan and cover with plastic wrap. Raise until the dough is 1 inch over the top of the bread pan.

8. Bake for 45 minutes, or until the internal temperature is 200 degrees and the outside is golden brown.

9. Rub the bread with butter if desired–the butter keeps the crust soft. Place the bread on its side on a wire rack to cook to keep the loaf from falling–if it lasts that long. We love to eat it when it is warm!

Makes 2 9-inch loaves

Honey

Since honey is produced from the nectar of flowers, honey will take on different flavors depending which flowers were used to produce it.

Perfect Whole-Wheat Bread

My three-year-old son asked for a slice of this bread. He is a very picky eater so Mom was thrilled he wanted something healthy. She cut him a slice and asked him if he wanted butter or jam on it. He replied, "No, this is very special bread. This doesn't need butter or jam." He knew how to make his grandma smile.

6 cups of hot water	5 tablespoons of lecithin granules
2/3 cup of honey	2 tablespoons of plain yogurt
2 tablespoons of salt	3 tablespoons of yeast
2/3 cup of coconut oil	14 to 15 1/2 cups of whole-wheat flour (about 10 cups of wheat kernels)

 Tip:

If possible grind the flour right before making it. Fresh flour is always better and healthier.

1. Combine water, honey, salt, oil, lecithin, and yogurt in a bread mixer or bowl and blend together.

2. Add 2 cups of flour and knead for a couple minutes. Add the yeast.

3. Continue to add the flour 1 cup at a time until the dough pulls away from the sides of the bowl.

4. Knead the dough for 10 minutes.

5. Let the dough rest for 5 to 10 minutes.

6. Divide the dough into 2 loaves.

7. Oil your hands and pound each section on the counter to get the air bubbles out. Roll each section into a ball and place each ball in a pan.

8. Place the dough in an oven set at 170 degrees. Let the dough rise until it rises about 1 inch over the top of the pan.

9. Turn the oven to 350 degrees. Leave the bread in the oven and bake for 25 minutes.

10. Remove the bread from the oven. Rub some butter on the top if desired and cool on cooling racks.

Makes two 1 ¹/₂-pound loaves, or two 2-pound loaves and a mini loaf.
Weight is measured before cooking.

Garlic Parmesan Baguettes

This is a tasty bread. It goes especially well with soup!

2 cups of warm water (about 110 degrees)

2 tablespoons of honey

2 tablespoons of yeast

2 teaspoons of salt

2 tablespoons of olive oil

5 to 6 cups of whole-grain flour (We add $^3/_4$ cup of white flour. The recipe would work great without it.)

2 tablespoons of butter, melted (olive oil is wonderful, too!)

1 to 2 garlic cloves, minced

Fresh Parmesan cheese, grated

 Tip:

Our flour mixture has spelt, wheat, Kamut®, and a small amount of quinoa (about $^1/_2$ cup) ground together.

1. In a bread mixer or bowl, pour in the water, honey, and yeast. Don't stir. Let the mixture sit for 10 minutes or until it starts to bubble.

2. Mix with bread mixer or by hand, adding the salt, oil, and about $^1/_2$ cup of flour at a time. (We add in half of the flour and let it sit for 5 to 10 minutes to let it sponge.) Knead, adding the rest of the flour until the dough pulls away from the bowl. The dough should be sticky to the touch. Knead the dough for about 5 minutes or until smooth.

3. Place in a bowl that has a small amount of oil at the bottom. Turn the dough until it is covered with oil. Cover the bowl with plastic wrap and let the dough double in size.

4. Rub a small amount of flour on your hands so the dough won't stick to them. Punch the dough down and then separate evenly into 4 sections.

5. Preheat oven to 400 degrees.

6. Roll the dough into long ropes and then twist them, if desired (this gives the baguettes a fun look). Let them rise for 30 minutes.

7. While the baguettes rise, mix the melted butter and garlic together in a small bowl and set aside. Bake the baguettes in the oven for about 12 to15 minutes, or until slightly golden.

8. Remove from the oven and make small slits in the bread, about 1 inch apart. Rub the garlic butter on top and in the slits. Grate the cheese on top and then place the bread back in the oven for another 3 minutes to heat the butter and melt the cheese. Serve warm.

Makes 4 baguettes

Parmesan

Parmesan cheese, or more officially "Parmigiano-Reggiano," is named for the areas of Italy that produce it. It is delicious on everything!

Sweet Challah Bread

This is a traditional Jewish braided bread with a nice flavor.

2 cups of warm water	3 teaspoons of salt
½ cup of honey	¼ cup of honey
2 tablespoons of yeast	8 cups of whole-grain flour
2 cups of whole-grain flour	1 egg
½ cup of coconut oil or olive oil	1 tablespoon of water
4 eggs	Sesame seeds, flax, poppy seeds, cheese, or cinnamon and sugar

1. In a bowl, pour in the water, honey, and yeast. Let it stand for about 10 minutes.

2. Stir in 2 cups of flour and cover it with a towel. Let stand for 30 minutes.

3. Add the egg and oil and beat until mixed.

4. Stir in the salt, honey, and the rest of the flour. (You want the dough to be sticky, so don't add too much flour.)

5. Knead by a machine for 5 to 8 minutes or by hand for 10 minutes. The dough should still be sticky.

6. Place the dough in an oiled bowl and turn until covered. Cover with a towel and let rise until double. (Or you can let rise overnight in the refrigerator.)

 **Tip:**

I use a mixture of spelt, Kamut®, brown rice, and oat flour.

7. Divide the dough into 3 equal portions to braid. A scale is helpful to balance the dough out evenly.

8. Roll each piece into a long rope. Connect the three pieces at the top and braid the bread. You can make the dough into a long braid or a circle. Place on parchment paper on a cookie sheet.

9. Beat together 1 egg and 1 tablespoon of water. Brush $1/2$ of the egg mixture on the top of the bread. Cover the bread with plastic and let it rise until double (this will take about 1 to 1 $1/2$ hours). Take off the plastic and brush on the remaining egg mixture.

10. Sprinkle the bread with the topping of your choice.

11. Preheat oven to 375 degrees. Bake the bread for 30 to 40 minutes, making sure to cover the bread with foil for the last 15 minutes if it starts getting too brown.

Makes 1 loaf

Lunch

Shrimp Salad with Brown Rice

This recipe is a nice combination of vegetables and shrimp and is easy to make. For a fun meal, put this mixture into whole-grain taco shells or tortillas.

1 $\frac{1}{2}$ pounds of frozen shrimp, cooked, shelled, and deveined

1 tablespoon of oil

$\frac{1}{3}$ cup of water

$\frac{1}{4}$ to $\frac{1}{2}$ teaspoon of chili powder

2 to 3 cups of cooked brown rice

1 to 1 $\frac{1}{2}$ cups of chopped coleslaw or cut up cabbage

1 avocado, chopped

$\frac{1}{4}$ cup of purple onion, chopped

2 Roma tomatoes, chopped

Chili powder to taste

1 teaspoon of salt

2 teaspoons of fresh lime juice

1. Heat the skillet with oil. Add the shrimp, water, and chili powder and heat for just a couple of minutes (don't do more than warm them or the shrimp will become tough). Add salt after cooking and set the pan aside, uncovered.

2. In individual bowls, place $1/2$ cup of cooked brown rice, then 6 to 7 shrimp on top, then $1/4$ cup of coleslaw or cabbage, then chopped avocados, onion, and tomatoes. Sprinkle chili powder on top if desired, along with a little salt and fresh lime juice. Enjoy!

Makes 4 to 5 servings

Whole-Grain Tortilla Pizza

This is a simple recipe with lots of options for using fresh vegetables. Let everyone make their own if that works for your family. Use the Whole-Grain Tortilla recipe on page 80 for the freshest ingredients.

3 tomatoes, chopped

$^1/_2$ of a purple onion, chopped

$^1/_2$ of a large yellow bell pepper, sliced

1 can of refried beans (we add chili verde) or any beans

$^1/_2$ teaspoon of cumin

$^1/_2$ teaspoon of chili powder

salt and pepper to taste

2 tablespoons of olive oil or grapeseed oil

$^1/_4$ cup of parmesan cheese

16 fresh basil leaves

4 whole-grain tortillas

1. Preheat oven to 375 degrees. Combine the vegetables with spices, salt, pepper, and oil in a bowl.

2. Place the tortillas on a cookie sheet. Scoop the beans on the tortilla and spread. Scoop the vegetables on top of the beans.

3. Sprinkle on the cheese and basil leaves. Bake until hot–about 3 to 5 minutes. Serve hot.

Makes 4 personal pizzas

The Tortilla

The tortilla is a staple food throughout much of North and South America. This famous flatbread has a close cousin in South Asia: the roti.

The Scoop on Beans

Some Benefits to Beans

1. They are cheap.

2. They are a great way to get fiber in your diet.

3. They are loaded with vitamins, minerals, and lots of complex carbohydrates.

4. One cup of most cooked beans contains $\frac{1}{2}$ the US daily recommendation of folic acid and Vitamin B.

5. Beans also contain magnesium, copper, potassium, and zinc.

Ways to Help Beans Digest Better

We have a missing enzyme called alpha-galactosidase that helps break down raffinose sugars that cause gas. Here are some techniques that might help reduce gas.

1. Drinking kefir every day helps foods digest easier.

2. Eating more beans may help. Start slowly. We need to eat beans often for our system to get use to them.

3. Don't eat beans with cabbage, brussel sprouts, or broccoli. These foods are harder to digest.

4. Some people think lentils, black-eyed peas, limas, chickpeas, and white beans digest easier. Start cooking with those first.

5. Don't cook beans in the water they soaked in. The water has a lot of the sugars in it.

6. Cook beans thoroughly. This technique makes them easier to digest.

7. Mix $\frac{1}{8}$ teaspoon of baking soda to the soaking water. It can help reduce the raffinose sugars you intake.

8. When using canned beans, drain and rinse them. This technique can help get rid of the raffinose sugar and $\frac{1}{2}$ of the unwanted sodium.

Turkey and Pesto on Sourdough

Make your own pesto sandwich at home! Mom says pesto is good enough to eat plain. This recipe would be a fantastic way to use leftovers from a turkey dinner.

2 tablespoons of oil

$1/2$ of a purple onion, sliced thin

1 clove of garlic, minced

$1/2$ to 1 pound of shredded turkey

$1/2$ cup of pesto

2 $1/2$ tablespoons of mayonnaise (optional)

Provolone cheese or other cheese preference

Oil for frying

8 slices of sourdough bread

1. In a small frying pan, heat the oil on medium heat and add the onions. Sauté for about 3 minutes. Stir in the garlic and sauté until the garlic is soft and tender.

2. Stir in the turkey and cook for about 2 more minutes. Remove from heat and set aside.

3. Blend the pesto with the mayonnaise, if desired. Spread the pesto on each slice of bread.

4. Scoop about $1/3$ cup of the turkey mixture on one side of the sandwich. Place provolone cheese on top, followed by the other piece of bread.

5. Heat a skillet to medium-high heat. With a small amount of oil, grill the sandwich on both sides until the cheese melts.

6. Serve warm with fresh fruit and vegetables.

Makes 4 sandwiches

Teriyaki Chicken Berry Salad

The combination of berries and teriyaki is surprisingly good. It is a wonderful summer meal.

$1/3$ cup of low sodium soy sauce

$1/4$ cup of water

2 tablespoons of honey

$1/4$ cup of orange juice

2 cloves of garlic, minced

1 tablespoon of fresh ginger, grated and peeled

3 chicken breasts, cut into pieces

$1 1/2$ to 2 cups of fresh blueberries

1 cup of fresh or frozen strawberries, sliced

2 cups of romaine lettuce, washed and torn into small pieces, or spinach

3 cups of cooked brown rice

1. In a small bowl, mix the soy sauce, water, honey, orange juice, garlic, and ginger. Set aside.

2. Place the chicken into a glass baking dish and pour the sauce over it, turning the chicken to make sure it is covered.

3. Cover and refrigerate for at least 2 hours.

4. On a barbecue, grill the chicken, making sure not to overcook it. Save the extra sauce.

5. Cook the extra sauce on medium-low heat (you could add $1/2$ teaspoon of cornstarch if the sauce needs thickening). Cool. Pour the berries into a bowl with the chicken and then add the sauce. Toss until the chicken and berries are covered.

6. Lightly toss in the lettuce. Serve over brown rice.

Serves 6 to 8

Pesto Pasta
with Shrimp

Leave this pasta plain or mix in spinach to make it more of a salad. It is a fun combination.

1-pound package of whole-grain pasta

1 tablespoon of oil

1 pound of shelled and deveined shrimp, cooked

$^3/_4$ cup of pesto

3 to 4 cloves of garlic, minced

1 15-ounce can of chickpeas, drained and rinsed (optional)

4 Roma tomatoes, chopped in small pieces

Salt and freshly ground pepper to taste

Fresh spinach (optional)

1. In a large pot, cook the pasta al dente. Add shrimp during the last 3 to 5 minutes of cooking and cook together.

2. Drain the shrimp and pasta. Add pesto, garlic, chickpeas, and tomatoes. Stir together. Add salt and pepper to taste. Serve on top of fresh spinach.

Serves 8

 Tip:

Add 1 tablespoon of oil to the water when boiling the pasta. This technique helps it to not boil over.

Whole-Grain Pasta

Pasta comes in a variety of shapes, colors, and flavors, including—wouldn't you know it—whole wheat! Whole-wheat pasta is often darker in color, and is usually available at normal grocery stores.

Chicken and Grain Pot Stickers

It's become our family tradition to gather on Super Bowl Sunday. We skip the football game and focus on family time and food. These potstickers were a great addition to our fun last year.

Filling

2 ¹/₂ cups of Napa cabbage

¹/₂ pound of ground chicken

2 garlic cloves minced

¹/₄ cup of water

1 tablespoon of low sodium soy sauce

2 tablespoons of Ultra Gel® or
1 tablespoon of cornstarch

1 tablespoon of fresh ginger, grated

³/₄ teaspoon of white pepper

¹/₄ teaspoon of mustard powder

¹/₂ cup of spelt berries, cooked rice, or cooked quinoa and 2 tablespoons of water

Sauce

2 tablespoons of soy sauce

2 tablespoons of rice vinegar

4 tablespoons of salsa

6 tablespoons of cilantro, chopped

4 cloves of garlic, minced

1 tablespoon of fresh ginger, grated

Assembly and Cooking

40 wonton wraps

Small bowl of water

Oil to cook them in (I use grapeseed oil)

Water

1. Mix ingredients for the sauce in a bowl and set the mixture aside. Cut up the cabbage into thin slices. Sprinkle the slices with salt and set them aside for 20 minutes (this will help get some of the moisture out).

2. Squeeze the cabbage in your fists over a bowl to get out the excess water.

3. In a skillet, sauté the chicken and garlic until lightly browned.

4. Place the cabbage, cooked meat, water, soy sauce, Ultra Gel® or cornstarch, ginger, pepper, mustard, and grain (if desired) in a blender or food processor. Blend the ingredients until combined and creamy.

5. Lay out the wonton wraps several at a time so you can make a production line. Scoop about a teaspoon of the cabbage mixture onto the center of each wonton wrapper.

6. Fill a small bowl with water. Wet your finger in the bowl and rub a little water all along the edge of each wonton wrapper. Fold each wrapper over to make a half-circle and seal it shut, squeezing out the air.

7. In a skillet, heat 2 tablespoons of oil to medium heat. Fill the skillet with the pot stickers, placed seam up and not touching. Lightly brown the potstickers on the bottom, then carefully pour in $1/3$ cup of water. Quickly cover the skillet and reduce heat to medium low. (Be careful when adding the water. If your oil is too hot, it could splatter.)

8. Cook until the water almost evaporates. Remove finished potstickers from the skillet and keep warm while you prepare the next batch. Wipe out the pan after each batch with a paper towel and restart the process.

9. Serve with the dipping sauce.

Makes about 35 small pot stickers

Sweet and Spicy Barley

While barley is a well-known grain, it's not one most people use in their diet. This recipe utilizes it in a way beyond the traditional barley soup.

1 tablespoon of coconut oil

$1/2$ onion, chopped in thin slices

2 cloves of garlic, minced

$3/4$ cup of uncooked barley (you could replace $1/4$ cup with quinoa, if desired)

$3 3/4$ cups of water

2 teaspoons of salt

2 teaspoons of thyme

$1/2$ to 1 teaspoon of finely chopped chipotle pepper or 1 to 1 $1/2$ teaspoons of chili powder (or a little of both if you like it extra spicy)

$1/3$ cup of uncooked brown rice

1 teaspoon of honey

$3/4$ cup of coarsely chopped walnuts

2 cups of fresh spinach

$1/2$ cup of dried cranberries

1. In a medium saucepan, sauté garlic and onion in coconut oil for 3 to 5 minutes, or until soft.

2. Add in the barley and quinoa and brown a little for about 3 minutes, stirring continually.

3. Stir in water, salt, thyme, peppers, and brown rice. Bring it to a boil and let it boil for about 2 minutes.

4. Turn the heat down to simmer and cook for an additional 45 to 60 minutes, until most of the water is absorbed and the grains are softened (don't stir too much or it will turn mushy).

5. In a small skillet, heat honey and walnuts until lightly toasted, about 3 to 4 minutes. Remove from heat and cool slightly, then drain in a strainer. Cool completely.

6. Toss the grains with spinach and top with walnuts and cranberries. Serve immediately.

Serves 6

Barley

Barley is commonly recognized as an ingredient in some kinds of alcohol. Not surprisingly, Ukraine, Germany, Russia, and France–known for their love of alcohol–are also the world's four largest barley producers.

Whole-Grain Tortillas

Mom's friend Jeanie told her about making tortillas at home. She got excited about it because she has been disappointed by the taste, the price, and the ingredients in the "healthy" ones. So she bought an electric tortilla maker and tried it out. It took a few attempts, but practice paid off. They tasted good, were truly healthy, and were even low-gluten. We make these frequently.

2 cups of whole-grain flour

1/2 teaspoon of salt

1/2 teaspoon of baking powder

2 tablespoons of olive oil

1 cup of warm water

1. Mix dry ingredients in a medium bowl.

2. Add the oil and water. Mix together until combined. Knead the mixture lightly, adding more flour as necessary. Put oil on your hands to keep the dough from sticking.

3. Let dough sit for 30 minutes.

4. Form the dough into walnut-sized balls (put oil on your hands again for this step.) Keep the dough really moist. Roll each ball out and cook on a griddle, pan, or tortilla maker.

Makes 8 tortillas

 *Tip:*

I grind 5 cups of spelt, 2 cups of Kamut®, 1 cup of brown rice, and 1 cup of oats for my flour.

How to Make Spelt Berries

Pressure Cooker Method

1. Pour 1 cup of spelt, 2 cups of water, and 1 tablespoon of coconut oil into the pressure cooker.

2. Set the pressure cooker on to high pressure. Set timer for 25 minutes.

3. Put on the lid and let it cook. Let the pressure release on its own. You can leave it on warm and serve whenever you want.

Stove Top Method

1. Pour 3 cups of water into a medium saucepan. Heat to a boil.

2. Pour 1 cup of spelt in the boiling water and add 1 tablespoon of coconut oil. Let it come to a boil again.

3. Put the lid on and turn it to low. Let it cook 40 to 60 minutes or until the spelt is soft and the grains start to split. Drain off the remaining water.

Oats

The largest producer of oats in the world is the European Union, followed by Russia, Canada, and Australia.

Granola

We love the "clumping factor" of this granola. It's a healthy alternative to the cold cereal my dad and brother love to eat.

$2/3$ cup of honey	1 cup of sunflower seeds
$1/2$ cup of coconut oil	1 cup of unsweetened coconut
3 cups of old-fashioned oats	1 teaspoon of cinnamon
1 cup of almonds, coarsely chopped	$1/2$ teaspoon of fresh ground nutmeg
$1/4$ cup of sesame seeds	Dried fruit, raisins, dates, craisins, if desired

1. Preheat oven to 250 degrees.

2. Melt the honey and oil in a small saucepan. Set aside.

3. Mix the dry ingredients. Pour in the honey mixture and stir until combined.

4. Line a cookie sheet with parchment paper. Pour the granola onto the cookie sheet (it will be thick).

5. Bake for 30 minutes. Stir the granola a couple of times during cooking.

6. Cool completely, then store in an air-tight container.

Makes 5 cups

Whole-Grain Fruit Bars

Whenever Mom makes these bars, our family enjoys them a lot! They have an excellent mixture of grains.

For the Crust and Topping

2 $\frac{1}{2}$ cups of whole-grain flour

$\frac{3}{4}$ cup of honey or 1 cup of sugar

2 $\frac{1}{4}$ cups of old-fashioned oats

1 teaspoon of salt

1 teaspoon of baking powder

$\frac{3}{4}$ teaspoon of baking soda

1 $\frac{1}{2}$ teaspoons of cinnamon

1 teaspoon of nutmeg

1 cup of coconut oil

For the Fruit Filling

$\frac{1}{4}$ cup of honey or $\frac{1}{3}$ cup of brown sugar

1 tablespoon of lemon zest

$\frac{1}{2}$ teaspoon of cinnamon

2 tablespoons of whole-grain flour or $\frac{1}{2}$ tablespoon of Ultra Gel®

1 $\frac{1}{2}$ cups of berries of your choice (we use boysenberries)

1 teaspoon of lemon juice

$\frac{1}{2}$ cup of water

2 tablespoons of butter

1. Preheat oven to 350 degrees. Grease a 9x13-inch pan and line it with parchment paper that extends up the sides of the pan.

2. In a medium-sized bowl, pour all the ingredients for the crust and topping. With a pastry blender or a fork and knife, cut in the honey and oil until crumbly. Reserve 2 cups of the mixture for the topping. Press the remaining dough into the bottom of the pan lined with parchment paper (make sure it touches all the way to the sides). Bake the crust until lightly golden, about 15 minutes.

3. While the crust is baking, pour all of the ingredients for the filling into a medium saucepan and cook until the mixture thickens, about 5 to 10 minutes.

4. When the crust is finished baking, pour the thickened filling on top. Crumble the remaining flour mixture on top of the filling. Bake for another 30 minutes, or until lightly golden.

5. Cool and serve.

Serves 8

Tip:

For my flour, I use 1 cup of spelt, 1 cup of Kamut®, $1/2$ cup of quinoa, $1/2$ cup of brown rice, and $1/2$ cup of amaranth. I have flour left over.

Almond Butter Oatmeal Puffs

There used to be some yummy treats called Peanut Butter Puffs Mom made when she was younger. They had peanut butter, Special K® cereal, sugar, and corn syrup. Mom wanted to make a healthier version of them and we loved the end result. They are quick and easy to make. You can add raisins, chocolate chips, or coconut, if desired.

$1/2$ cup of almond butter

1 cup of old-fashioned oatmeal

$1/4$ cup of honey

1 teaspoon of vanilla

Granola

1. In a large bowl, mix the almond butter, honey, and oatmeal until combined. Stir in the vanilla.

2. Form the mixture into small balls, and roll each ball in the granola. Eat immediately, or save for later in an air-tight container in the refrigerator or freezer.

Makes 6 to 8 puffs

Graham Cracker Bites

These are a graham cracker rolled up into a cookie. They are soft in the middle and a healthy alternative.

2 cups of spelt flour	¹/₂ teaspoon of cinnamon
1 cup of oat flour	3 tablespoons of honey
¹/₂ cup of sugar	²/₃ cup of coconut oil
1 teaspoon of baking soda	3 tablespoons of almond milk

1. Preheat oven to 350 degrees. Grease a cookie sheet.

2. In a large bowl, combine the dry ingredients.

3. In a small saucepan, heat the honey and oil for 30 seconds. Stir until combined.

4. Add the honey mixture into the dry ingredients. Stir in the milk until combined.

5. Roll the graham cracker mixture into balls and place on the greased cookie sheet.

6. Bake for 8 to 10 minutes.

Makes 2 dozen bites

Rolled Power Bars

A lot of food that is advertised as healthy is not very healthy at all. Read the labels and you'll find a lot of processed ingredients. It's cheaper and often healthier to make your own.

3 cups of dates

4 cups of 6-grain rolled oats or old-fashioned oats

1 cup of unsweetened coconut

$1/4$ cup of chia (optional)

$1/4$ cup of flax, ground

$1/4$ cup of cashews, chopped fine

$1/4$ cup of almonds, chopped fine

$1/4$ cup of sesame seeds

$1/4$ cup of pumpkin seeds

2 tablespoons of peanut butter

$1/2$ cup of coconut oil

2 tablespoons of cinnamon

$1/2$ teaspoon of salt

1. Place the dates in a bowl and cover with water. Soak for 20 to 30 minutes, or until the dates are soft.

2. Drain the water into another bowl. Pour the dates into the blender and blend into a paste. Add some of the water you drained off to help make the paste if your dates did not absorb enough liquid. (You don't want it to be runny, so add a little at a time.)

3. Pour the date mixture and all the remaining ingredients into an empty bowl. Mix until combined. Roll the mixture into balls, place the balls on a cookie sheet, and harden in the freezer.

Makes 28 balls

Raw Almond Butter Treats

These store wonderfully in the freezer in a zipper-topped bag or air-tight container.

5 to 6 dates, softened

$^1/_4$ cup of almond butter (or peanut butter)

$^1/_2$ cup of old-fashioned oats

$^1/_3$ cup of pumpkin seeds, unsalted

$^1/_3$ cup of cashew pieces, unsalted

2 tablespoons of coconut oil

1. Place the dates in a bowl and cover with water. Soak for 20 to 30 minutes, or until the dates are soft, and drain.

2. Pour all of the ingredients into the blender and pulse for a couple of seconds. Stir. Continue pulsing and stirring until the mixture sticks together.

3. Form the mixture into small balls. Place the balls on a cookie sheet and harden in the freezer or refrigerator (you can eat them soft, too).

Makes 6 treats

 Tip:

If you don't have time to soak the dates, you can put them in the microwave with a little water for 30 seconds.

Granola with a Tropical Twist

We enjoy trying different versions of granola, and we love the twist of tropical fruit and applesauce in this one. The dried fruit blend we use has mango, blueberries, and cranberries.

3 cups of 6-grain rolled oats	4 tablespoons of sugar and cinnamon, blended
$^1/_3$ cup of applesauce	1 cup of cashew pieces
$^1/_3$ cup of water	1 cup of dried tropical fruit blend
	$^1/_2$ cup of unsweetened coconut flakes

1. Preheat oven to 325 degrees.

2. Mix all of the ingredients together.

3. Pour the granola onto a cookie sheet lined with parchment paper.

4. Bake for 30 minutes. Stir the granola a couple of times during cooking.

5. Cool completely, then store in an air-tight container.

Makes 4 cups of granola

 Tip:

If you can't find 6-grain rolled oats, you can substitute with old-fashioned oats.

Sides & Salads

Apple, Almond, and Feta Salad with Honey Chia Dressing

This fantastic salad is one of our favorites and sure to be a crowd pleaser.

Dressing

$1/2$ cup of honey

2 tablespoons of chia

$3/4$ cup of grapeseed oil or another kind of oil

$1/2$ cup of apple cider vinegar

$1/4$ teaspoon of pepper

Salad

1 head of Romaine lettuce, washed and torn in small pieces

1 cup of chopped almonds

2 tablespoons of honey

2 green apples cut in small bite-sized pieces

$1/2$ cup of dried cranberries

$1/2$ red onion diced in small pieces

4 ounces of feta cheese, crumbled

1. Combine the dressing ingredients in a blender or shaker bottle. Refrigerate the dressing until serving.

2. Heat almonds and honey in a saucepan over medium heat until thick. Remove from heat.

3. Just before serving, toss almonds with lettuce, apples, cranberries, and onion. Lightly mix in the cheese.

4. Serve with dressing on the side.

Serves 6

Chia

Despite its health benefits (chia is rich in omega-3 fatty acids), the first major use of chia in the United States was actually the Chia Pet, a novelty gift that rose to popularity in the 1980s.

Quinoa Fruit Salad

A great-tasting fruit salad with a little bit of grain crazy. You could also use a flavored yogurt in place of the plain.

2 cups of water	2 tablespoons of freshly squeezed orange juice
$1/8$ teaspoon of salt	$1/2$ teaspoon of orange zest
1 cup of quinoa, rinsed thoroughly	2 kiwis, peeled and chopped in small pieces
$1/3$ cup of fresh mint, chopped finely	1 can (11 ounces) mandarin oranges, drained
$1/4$ cup of plain yogurt	1 can (14 ounces) pineapple tidbits, drained
1 tablespoon of honey	5 strawberries, chopped in small pieces
	$3/4$ cup of fresh blueberries

 *Tip:*

Quinoa can sometimes have a bitter taste if it is not rinsed off. Run water over it in a strainer when preparing it.

1. Bring water and salt to a boil. Add the quinoa.

2. Lower to a simmer, cover, and cook for about 15 minutes, or until the quinoa is tender.

3. Drain and rinse the quinoa and set aside.

4. In a blender, combine the mint, yogurt, orange juice, and zest. Pulse until blended.

5. Prepare the fruit. Mix the fruit with the yogurt mixture.

6. Add the quinoa and toss gently.

Serves 6

Barley Quinoa Pilaf

This is a fantastic-looking pilaf and it tastes delicious. Instead of a basic pilaf, which uses nutrient-empty white rice, this recipe is full of whole grains and vegetables.

$1/2$ cup of grapeseed oil or olive oil

$1/2$ of a white onion, finely chopped

$3/4$ cup of chopped leek or green onion

1 cup of barley

$1/2$ cup of quinoa

2 teaspoons of chicken seasoning

$2 3/4$ cups of water (you could use chicken broth)

1 to 1 $1/4$ cups of shredded carrots

1 can (14 ounces) of sliced mushrooms
or
1 $1/2$ cups of fresh mushrooms

$1/4$ cup of green onion chopped for garnish

Salt and pepper to taste

Pine nuts (optional)

1. Preheat oven to 350 degrees.

2. Heat the oil in a skillet over medium heat and sauté the onions and leeks until soft.

3. Stir in the barley and quinoa and cook for 5 minutes.

4. Pour into a covered baking dish and stir in the chicken seasoning, 1 $1/2$ cups of water, and carrots. Bake for 30 minutes.

5. Remove from oven and stir in the remaining 1 $1/4$ cups of water. Cover and bake for another 30 minutes.

6. Remove from oven and garnish with green onions and pine nuts, if desired. Enjoy!

Serves 6

Grain on Hand

Make a large amount of the brown rice mix and keep the leftovers in the refrigerator for other meals. It stays good for a week and is a great way to add grains to other meals or create a quick side dish.

Basic Brown Rice Mix

We usually keep the ratio of brown rice to other grains around 2 to 1.

2 cups of brown rice

1 cup of barley or $1/2$ cup of barley and
$1/2$ cup of quinoa or $1/2$ cup of barley and $1/2$ cup of millet

6 cups of water

Spices of your choice (we like marjoram, basil, or cilantro)

1. Cook the brown rice in a pressure cooker, rice cooker, or on the stovetop like ordinary rice. Rice is done when soft and tender.

Serves 6

Entrées

Homemade Hamburgers

Pre-made patties are not as good as the ones you make yourself. This recipe cooks for a crowd, but you can always freeze individually wrapped patties to save them for later. Make with our Whole-Grain Hamburger Buns on page 50.

2 cups of whole-grain bread crumbs (we use 3 pieces of whole-grain toast)

1 pound natural ground turkey chub

3 pounds of natural lean ground beef

1 egg, beaten

1 teaspoon of dry mustard

2 teaspoons of steak seasoning

3 tablespoons of dried minced onion

3 tablespoons of Worcestershire sauce

1 teaspoon of salt

$1/4$ teaspoon of pepper

Hamburger buns and toppings

1. In a big bowl, combine all the ingredients (except the buns and toppings).

2. Form the meat into patties.

3. Grill the patties, cooking each side only once. Top with a slice of cheese, if desired, while the second side cooks.

4. Load onto a whole-grain hamburger bun with your favorite toppings and enjoy!

Makes 16 patties

The Hamburger

From Tulsa, Oklahoma, to Hamburg, Germany, there are at least seven competing claims for the origin of the hamburger. We don't know who did it, but we're sure glad they did!

Asian Turkey Wraps in Romaine Lettuce

It is easy to get in a rut eating the same fruits and vegetables with the same narrow window of nutrients. Romaine lettuce has some surprising health benefits that make this recipe a great one for any family.

1 tablespoon of oil (I use grape-seed oil)

1 ½ pounds of lean ground turkey

1 jalapeño pepper, seeded and diced

1 can (4 ounce) of diced green chilies

3 to 4 cloves of garlic, minced

2 teaspoons of lime zest

3 tablespoons of fresh lime juice

5 tablespoons of fish sauce

2 tablespoons of honey or brown sugar

2 cups of cooked brown rice

1 teaspoon of cornstarch or 1 table-spoon of Ultra Gel®

¼ cup of fresh basil, chopped

4 green onions, chopped

2 heads of Romaine lettuce, washed and separated from hull

1. Heat the oil in a frying pan. Add turkey and brown.

2. Stir in the peppers, chilies, garlic, and zest and cook for a couple of minutes.

Romaine Lettuce

Some of the nutrients in this vegetable include:

1. Vitamin C and beta carotene, which aid in a healthy heart by preventing oxidation of cholesterol.

2. Folic acid, which keeps blood vessels healthy.

3. Potassium, which helps lower blood pressure and improves muscle strength when combined with strength training.

4. Fiber, which improves the functioning of our bodies and helps burn fat.

5. Phosphorus, calcium, and magnesium.

3. In a small bowl, whisk lime juice, fish sauce, honey, rice, and cornstarch or Ultra Gel®. Add mixture to frying pan and cook until thickened.

4. Remove from heat and add basil and green onions.

5. Serve filling with lettuce on the side. Scoop filling into individual leaves of lettuce as you eat.

Serves 6

Brown Rice with Herbs, Chicken, and Vegetables

This dish has beautiful color. Mom says, "It makes me happy inside just looking at it."

3 boneless chicken breasts

$1/4$ cup of water

2 cloves of garlic, minced

1 yellow onion, sliced

3 cups of cooked brown rice

1 cup of fresh spinach

1 cup of chopped carrots

$1/4$ cup of chopped cilantro

$1/4$ cup of fresh parsley

1 teaspoon of oregano

1 teaspoon of basil

1 teaspoon of thyme

Salt and pepper to taste

1. Place the chicken and water in a big pot on medium heat. Cover and cook for 10 minutes. Remove the lid and cut the chicken into small pieces (kitchen shears make this easy).

2. Add garlic and onion and cook another 3 minutes. Stir in the cooked rice. When the chicken is almost done, add the vegetables and herbs. Reduce heat, cover, and cook until carrots are soft. Salt and pepper it to taste.

3. Serve warm.

Serves 6

Citrus Salmon Stir Fry

While this citrus marinade could be used on meat or chicken, the grapefruit really complements the flavor of salmon.

$1/3$ cup of grapefruit juice

1 tablespoon of dried parsley or 2 tablespoons of fresh parsley

2 tablespoons of fresh lemon juice or lime juice

1 tablespoon of olive oil

1 teaspoon of dried thyme

2 cloves of garlic, minced

$1/4$ teaspoon of pepper

1 pound of salmon

2 tablespoons of coconut oil

1 bag (16 ounces) of broccoli, stir fry vegetables, or vegetables of your choosing

Cooked brown rice

Salt and pepper to taste

1. Mix the grapefruit juice, parsley, lemon juice, olive oil, thyme, garlic, and pepper in a bowl.

2. Place the fish in the bowl, cover with the marinade, and let sit for 20 minutes.

3. Melt the coconut oil in a frying pan on medium heat. Add the fish and the marinade.

4. Cook the fish on both sides. Add the vegetables and cover. Reduce heat to medium low and steam for 3 minutes.

5. Serve over brown rice.

Serves 4

Tom Kha Gai

This Thai soup is one of our favorites. The coconut, ginger, and lemongrass flavors are delicious and it's still hearty with its brown-rice base. You can find some of the more unusual ingredients at your local Asian market.

2 cans (13.5 ounces) of coconut milk

6 cups of chicken broth (I just use the water that I cook the chicken in)

$\frac{1}{2}$ teaspoon of salt

4 stalks of fresh lemongrass, washed well

6 red shallots, peeled and chopped

3 cloves of garlic, minced

1 teaspoon of coriander

2 handfuls of cilantro leaves

1 to 2 jalapeño peppers, seeded and chopped

2 tablespoons of fresh ginger or galangal, chopped

Zest from 1 lime

1 to 2 teaspoons of chili garlic sauce (optional)

3 cups of cooked chicken chopped into pieces (cooked in 6 cups of water to use for broth)

1 cup of chopped mushrooms

3 tablespoons of fish sauce

2 tablespoons of lime juice

1 handful of cilantro (optional)

6 cups of cooked brown rice

1. In a pot on medium-heat, combine the milk, broth, salt, lemongrass (do not chop these), shallots, garlic, coriander, cilantro, peppers, ginger, zest, and chili sauce. Cook for 15 minutes.

2. Remove the lemongrass and add the chicken, mushrooms, and fish sauce. Cook for another 10 minutes. Stir in the lime juice and another handful of cilantro if desired. Heat for 3 more minutes.

3. Serve over brown rice.

Serves 8

Barbecue Chicken Pizza

This is your basic homemade barbecue pizza, but the dough could be used for any variety of pizza. One of my sisters who was baking with us tried a variation with barbecue sauce, sun-dried tomatoes, and fresh basil, and it was deliciously sweet and savory.

Barbecue Sauce

$3/4$ cup of tomato sauce

$1/4$ cup of apple cider

$1/2$ cup of brown sugar or sugar substitute

1 tablespoon of Worcestershire sauce

1 tablespoon of soy sauce

$1 1/2$ teaspoons of honey

1 tablespoon of minced garlic

$1/4$ teaspoon of ground ginger

Pizza Dough

1 tablespoon of yeast

1 cup of warm water (around 110 degrees)

2 tablespoons of olive oil

2 tablespoons of sugar

$1 1/2$ cups of whole-wheat flour

$1 1/4$ cups of all-purpose flour

1 teaspoon of salt

Pizza

2 chicken breasts, cooked and shredded

$1/2$ cup of chopped red onions

$1/2$ cup of fresh cilantro

2 cups of grated mozzarella cheese

 Tip:

To shred chicken quickly and easily, put freshly cooked chicken in an electric mixer with the cookie paddles on.

1. Mix the sauce ingredients together in a small saucepan on medium heat for 20 minutes, or until thickened.

2. Reduce heat to low and allow the sauce to simmer while you make the dough (the longer the sauce simmers, the better the flavor).

3. Preheat oven to 425 degrees.

4. Mix the yeast, warm water, olive oil, and sugar together in an electric mixer or large bowl, and let stand for 5 minutes.

5. Mix in the dry ingredients, adding the flour gradually until the dough no longer sticks to the sides of the bowl. Knead for 5 minutes, then raise for 15 minutes.

6. Roll out the dough on a pizza pan to your desired thickness (we prefer a thicker crust at $1/4$ to $1/2$ inch thick). Bake the crust until golden brown.

7. Remove the crust from the oven and liberally spread on the barbecue sauce. Top with chicken, onions, cilantro, and cheese. Bake again until cheese melts.

Makes 1 pizza (12 small pieces).

🌾 Tip:

I mixed 2 $1/2$ cups of spelt, 1 cup of Kamut®, and $1/2$ cup of brown rice flour together and used 1 $1/4$ cups of that instead of all-purpose flour.

Butternut Squash and Shrimp Pasta

This combination tastes so yummy. The squash adds a natural creaminess to the pasta.

1 butternut squash (peeled and chopped in cubes)

2 to 3 tablespoons of oil

1 ¹/₂ teaspoons of salt

2 to 3 teaspoons of oil

1 onion, minced

5 cloves of garlic, minced

1 tablespoons of fresh or dried thyme

1 tablespoon of marjoram, minced (optional)

1 red pepper, minced

2 cups of water

1 tablespoon of cornstarch or Ultra Gel® (optional)

Lemon juice from 2 lemons

12 to 16 ounces of shrimp, peeled, cooked, and deveined

Salt and pepper to taste

1 package (12 ounces) of whole-grain pasta, cooked

Parsley, fresh or dried for garnish, if desired

1. Preheat oven to 350 degrees.

2. Place the cut-up squash in a bowl with the oil and toss until covered. Pour the squash on a cookie sheet and bake for 30 minutes, occasionally turning the squash pieces. Sprinkle with salt.

3. While the squash is cooking, sauté the onions with oil in a frying pan on medium heat. Add the garlic, herbs, and red pepper, and cook for 3 to 5 minutes.

4. Add water and cook on low for 8 to 10 minutes. If you want a thicker sauce, add cornstarch or Ultra Gel® at the end.

5. Remove from heat and stir in the lemon juice and shrimp. Cover and return to heat, allowing the shrimp to heat all the way through.

6. Toss the shrimp mixture with the roasted squash.

7. Serve over whole-grain pasta. Garnish with parsley if desired.

Serves 6

 Tip:

To easily juice a lemon, roll the lemon on the counter. Put the lemon in the microwave for 20 to 30 seconds. Remove, cut in half, and squeeze.

Sweet and Sour Chicken

This is another chance to make your own delicious sauce instead of being subject to whatever the food industry puts in the premade sauces you buy at the store.

Brown Rice

2 cloves of garlic

2 tablespoons of fresh marjoram

2 $\frac{1}{2}$ cups of brown rice

5 cups of water

Salt and pepper

Chicken and Sauce

1 $\frac{1}{2}$ pounds of chicken tenders

$\frac{1}{3}$ cup of soy sauce

1 cup of water

3 tablespoons of lemon juice

$\frac{1}{4}$ cup of honey

4 fresh basil leaves or 1 teaspoon of dried basil

3 cloves of garlic, minced

1 tablespoon of fresh ginger or

1 $\frac{1}{2}$ teaspoons of ground ginger

1 teaspoon of thyme

1 onion, chopped up fine

1 leek, cut in small pieces

1 orange pepper, chopped in small pieces

1. Mix the brown rice with the spices and cook in a pressure cooker or rice cooker according to the manufacturer's directions (you can also cook on the stovetop.)

2. While the rice is cooking, place the chicken in a large pan with $1/4$ cup of water. Cover and cook on medium-high for 3 minutes.

3. Uncover and stir in the remaining ingredients. Cover and cook on medium-low for another 30 minutes.

4. Cut the chicken into small pieces (kitchen shears make this easy).

5. Mix the sauce and chicken with the cooked rice. Salt and pepper as needed.

6. Serve.

Serves 4

Enchiladas

Mom always made creamy enchiladas when I was growing up, but we've since decided that red sauce enchiladas are a lot healthier. Use the Whole-Grain Tortillas from page 80.

Sauce

1 clove of garlic, minced

1 tablespoon of chipotle chilies in adobo sauce

1 1/2 cups of tomato sauce

1/4 teaspoon of chili powder

1/2 teaspoon of ground cumin

3/4 cup of fat free chicken broth

Salt and pepper to taste

Meat

1 teaspoon of olive oil

1/2 cup of diced onion

1 to 1 1/2 cups of shredded cooked chicken breast

1/4 cup of chopped fresh cilantro

1/3 cup of chicken broth

1/2 cup of tomato sauce

Other

1/2 package of Neufchatel cheese

6 tortillas

2 cups of shredded Mexican cheese mix

Fresh cilantro, chopped

1. Preheat oven to 400 degrees.

2. Lightly sauté the minced garlic in a large saucepan over medium heat. Add the chipotle chilies, tomato sauce, chili powder, cumin, chicken broth, and salt and pepper. Simmer for 10 minutes, then remove from heat.

3. In a medium saucepan, sauté the onions in olive oil until soft. Add chicken, cilantro, chicken broth, tomato sauce, and 2 large spoonfuls of the sauce you have already made. Simmer for 5 minutes.

4. Divide Neufchatel cheese into 6 even portions. Spread a portion on each tortilla and divide the chicken mixture evenly between the tortillas. Roll and place side by side in an 8x10-inch pan.

5. Pour the sauce mixture over the top of the tortillas and top with cheese. Cover the pan with foil and bake for 20 minutes. Remove the foil and bake for 5 more minutes, or until the cheese begins to bubble.

6. Top with fresh cilantro and serve.

Serves 6

Desserts

Strawberry Shortcake Bites

Strawberry shortcake already feels like a healthy dessert, but this takes it to a whole new, delicious level using spelt flour and whipped coconut milk for the cream.

Shortcake

2 cups of whole-grain flour (we use spelt)

1 teaspoon of baking powder

$^1/_2$ teaspoon of baking soda

$^1/_2$ teaspoon of salt

$^1/_4$ cup of strawberry puree

2 tablespoons of coconut oil, softened

1 cup of coconut or almond milk

1 teaspoon of vanilla

$^1/_2$ cup of honey

1 egg, beaten

Topping

1 can of coconut milk

4 tablespoons of powdered sugar

1 teaspoon of vanilla

Chopped strawberries

1. Chill the coconut milk (for topping) overnight in the refrigerator.

2. Preheat oven to 350 degrees. Grease the muffin tin.

3. In a small bowl, mix the dry ingredients.

4. In a large bowl, whisk the wet ingredients.

 **Tip:**

Ultra Gel® is one of my favorite food products. It's a corn starch that doesn't need any cooking and it doesn't clump together. It works perfectly to thicken fruit sauces, whipped cream, and hot liquids.

5. Gradually mix the dry ingredients into the wet ingredients until just combined.

6. Spoon mixture into the mini muffin tin, filling each about two-thirds full. Bake for 10 minutes, or until a toothpick inserted in the center comes out clean.

7. Allow muffins to cool in the tin for 5 to 10 minutes, then turn out onto a cooling rack.

8. Just before serving, whisk the chilled coconut milk, powdered sugar, and vanilla together until it starts to thicken (the coconut milk should already be thickened a bit from being in the refrigerator overnight.) Some varieties of coconut milk might not thicken as well; add a little Ultra Gel® or gelatin if necessary.

9. After the muffins have cooled, frost with the whipped coconut cream and top with chopped strawberries.

10. Serve immediately.

Makes 24 mini muffins

Strawberry Yogurt Kamut® Cake

This cake is made out of Kamut® flour. It turns out beautifully moist and is a wonderful breakfast and snack. The recipe uses no butter—only coconut oil—and it works great.

2 ½ cups of Kamut® flour (or another whole-grain flour)

½ teaspoon of baking soda

½ teaspoon of salt

¾ cup of coconut oil

1 cup of honey

3 eggs

3 tablespoons of fresh lemon juice

1 teaspoon of lemon zest (optional)

1 cup of plain yogurt or Greek yogurt

1 ½ cups of frozen strawberries

Powdered sugar

1. Preheat oven to 325 degrees. Grease and flour a Bundt pan.

2. In a medium bowl, sift together 2 ¼ cups of flour, baking soda, and salt. Stir in the zest and set aside.

3. In another bowl, beat the oil and honey until light and creamy. Beat in the eggs one at a time, then stir in the lemon juice. Gradually add the yogurt and flour into the oil mixture, alternating between yogurt and flour. Mix until combined, being careful not to overmix.

4. Chop the frozen berries into small pieces (a blender works well). Mix ¼ cup of remaining flour with the berries. Fold the berry-flour mixture into the batter.

5. Pour the cake batter into the Bundt pan and bake for 30 to 40 minutes until lightly golden brown, or until a toothpick inserted in the center comes clean.

6. Cool the cake for 10 minutes in the pan, then turn the cake out on a cooling rack.

7. Cool completely, dust with powdered sugar, and enjoy!

Serves 12

Almond Butter Quinoa Bites

This was an experiment that turned out well! We enjoy peanut butter bars, but we wanted to make a healthier version. The recipe is gluten-free, which is an added bonus.

1 cup of natural almond butter	1 $1/2$ cups of quinoa flour
$2/3$ cup of honey	1 teaspoon of baking powder
2 eggs	Dark chocolate chips, coconut, or dried fruit (optional)
1 teaspoon of vanilla	

1. Preheat oven to 350 degrees. Grease a 9x9-inch pan.

2. Combine the wet ingredients in a mixing bowl.

3. In a separate bowl, mix the dry ingredients. Add the wet ingredients to the dry and mix thoroughly.

4. Pour the mixture into the greased pan and bake for 20 minutes, or until a knife comes out clean.

5. Cool before serving for easier cutting.

Serves 6

Coconut Brown Rice Pudding with Currants

Currants are similar in taste to a raisin, but smaller and sweeter. This rice pudding makes a nice breakfast or light dessert.

2 cups of milk

$^2/_3$ cup of coconut milk

$^1/_4$ to $^1/_2$ cup of packed brown sugar or sweetener

$^1/_8$ teaspoon of salt

1 tablespoon of cornstarch

2 cups of cooked brown rice

2 eggs, beaten

1 teaspoon of cinnamon

$^1/_2$ teaspoon of freshly grated or $^1/_4$ teaspoon of ground nutmeg

2 teaspoons of orange zest (optional)

1 teaspoon of vanilla

Currants

1. Whisk milk, coconut milk, sugar, and cornstarch in a saucepan. Bring to a boil and stir in the rice.

2. Beat the eggs in a separate bowl. Stir $^1/_4$ cup of the hot mixture into the eggs. Then stir the egg mixture into the rest of the milk mixture in the saucepan. Reduce heat to low and continue stirring until mixture thickens. Stir in the spices. Add orange zest, if desired.

3. Remove pudding from heat and stir in the vanilla.

4. Serve topped with with currants, cinnamon, milk, or your favorite topping.

Serves 4

Brown Rice

Brown rice is chewier and healthier than ordinary white rice because it still has the bran and the germ fully intact (see diagram on page 2). White rice is created by removing these parts from the grain.

Oatmeal Cashew Chocolate Chip Cookies

Mom and I love the cookies at a local vegan sandwich shop, and Mom tried to mimic the recipe. The cashew powder adds a creaminess to the cookie, and they are full of healthy ingredients that we would not feel bad eating them for breakfast!

$^1/_2$ cup of almond or soy milk

2 tablespoons of apple cider vinegar

3 cups of whole-grain flour

$^1/_2$ teaspoon of salt

2 teaspoons of baking soda

$^1/_2$ cup of cashews

$^1/_2$ cup of coconut oil

1 $^1/_4$ to 1 $^1/_2$ cups of honey (depending on your sweetness preference) or 2 cups of sugar for vegan recipe

1 tablespoon of vanilla

6 cups of old-fashioned oatmeal

1 cup of chocolate chips or dried fruit or nuts

1. Preheat oven to 350 degrees.

2. In a small bowl, combine the milk and vinegar. Set aside for 10 minutes so the milk can curdle.

3. In a separate bowl, combine the flour, salt, and baking soda.

4. Grind the cashews in a blender until they become a powder.

5. In a large mixing bowl, beat the oil, honey, and cashew powder until creamy. Beat in the vanilla. Stir in the milk mixture.

6. Gradually add the flour mixture and oatmeal, alternating between the two. Fold in the chocolate chips.

7. Scoop the cookie dough in small spoonfuls onto a cookie sheet covered with parchment paper. Flatten gently.

8. Bake for 8 to 10 minutes, or until lightly golden brown.

9. Cool on cooling rack.

 Tip:

My flour mixture: 2 cups of Kamut®, 3/4 cup of spelt, and 1/4 cup of teff.

Cherry Chocolate Chip Oatmeal Cookies

Mom made these in an effort to make a granola-bar-like cookie. They are healthy and a treat! They would make a great addition to a school or work lunch—a touch of sweetness without the guilt.

$3/4$ cup of honey

1 $1/3$ cups of coconut oil

1 teaspoon of vanilla

1 teaspoon of almond extract

2 eggs

$1/4$ cup of almond butter

4 cups of whole-wheat flour (I use Kamut® flour)

1 teaspoon of baking soda

$1/2$ teaspoon of baking powder

$1/4$ teaspoon of salt

1 cup of rolled oats

1 cup of dried cherries (any dried fruit would do)

1 cup of shredded unsweetened coconut

$1/2$ cup of chocolate chips

1. Preheat oven to 350 degrees.

2. In a small saucepan over medium-low heat, melt honey and coconut oil until creamy.

3. In a large bowl, combine honey mixture with all other ingredients.

4. Form the mixture into 1–inch balls and place the balls on a cookie sheet. Flatten gently.

5. Bake for 10 minutes, or until lightly golden brown.

Makes 4 dozen

Khorasan Wheat

Kamut® flour is made from khorasan wheat. While the exact origin of this wheat is unknown, it is among the most ancient wheat varieties known. Turkish legend says that this is the same grain Noah carried on the ark, hence it is sometimes called "prophet's wheat."

Nectarine Berry Crumble

We had a large number of nectarines that needed to be used. We were in the mood to do some fall baking, so we came up with this recipe. It tastes great with whipped cream, ice cream, or almond milk.

7 cups of nectarines, peeled and chopped into bite–sized pieces

3 tablespoons of fresh orange juice (the juice from about one orange)

3 tablespoons of Kamut® flour or whole-grain flour

3 tablespoons of honey

1 ½ cups of blackberries or boysenberries

½ cup of whole-grain flour

¾ cup of coconut oil

2 cups of old–fashioned oatmeal

½ cup of brown sugar or other sweetener

½ teaspoon of nutmeg

1 teaspoon of cinnamon

½ teaspoon of baking powder

1. Preheat oven to 350 degrees. Grease a 9x13-inch pan.

2. In a bowl, mix together the nectarines, juice, flour, and honey. Fold in the berries. Pour the mixture into the greased 9x13–inch pan.

3. In another bowl, mix together flour, oil, oatmeal, brown sugar, nutmeg, cinnamon, and baking powder with a pastry blender until a crumbly mixture forms. Spread the mixture over the top of the fruit.

4. Bake for 20 to 30 minutes, until the fruit is tender. Enjoy with your favorite topping.

Serves 8

Oatmeal Chocolate Chip Cookie Tart

While not an exact replica, this recipe is inspired by the layered, holiday cookie made with Eagle brand milk. You can make it gluten free by using gluten-free oatmeal.

3 ¹/₄ cups of old-fashioned oatmeal

²/₃ cup of honey

¹/₃ cup of coconut oil or butter (melted)

2 teaspoons of cinnamon (optional)

³/₄ cup of dates, chopped

1 ¹/₄ cups of water

1 cup of almonds, chopped

¹/₂ cup of cashews, chopped

¹/₄ cup of unsweetened coconut

¹/₂ cup of dark chocolate chips

Chocolate chips and coconut (optional)

1. Preheat oven to 350 degrees. Grease a tart pan or pie pan.

2. Blend the oatmeal in a blender until it turns to flour. Pour into a bowl.

3. With a pastry blender, blend the honey and oil into the oatmeal flour. Add in the cinnamon, if desired. Press the mixture into the tart pan or pie pan. Make it thin, about ¹/₄ inch thick.

4. Bake for 10 minutes. Set finished crust aside.

 *Tip:*

Add ¹/₂ cup of honey to the date mixture if you want it sweeter. You could not blend ¹/₂ the oatmeal and have a more textured crust.

5. Pour the dates and water into a sauce pan and heat on medium heat until the dates turn soft. Stir in the nuts and coconut and cook for 3 minutes. Remove from heat.

6. Stir in the chocolate chips. Pour the mixture onto the crust and spread.

7. Garnish with chocolate chips and coconut, if desired.

8. Slice and serve.

Chocolate Chip Cookie Bars

With no flour or eggs, this is a different kind of recipe than you'd normally make. Your family will enjoy these thick, hearty, healthy cookies, and we promise that you won't even notice the beans!

1 cup of dates	3 tablespoons of coconut oil
Water	2 teaspoons of vanilla extract
1 teaspoon of baking soda	1/2 teaspoon of baking soda
2 cups of white beans, drained and rinsed	2 teaspoons of baking powder
3/4 cup of honey	1/4 teaspoon of salt
1 cup of old-fashioned oats	1 cup of chocolate chips

1. In a small container, cover the dates with hot water. Add 1 teaspoon of baking soda and give the dates a gentle stir. Let sit for a couple of hours.

2. Preheat oven to 350 degrees.

3. Rinse the dates thoroughly and pat dry. Blend the dates, white beans, and honey in a high-powered blender or food processor.

4. In a large bowl, mix the date mixture with the other ingredients. Mix in the chocolate chips.

5. Press the mixture into an 8x8-inch pan. Bake for 20 to 25 minutes. Cool before cutting and serving.

Serves 6

 Tip:

Soaking the dates in water and baking soda will soften the dates and keep them soft even after baking.

Volume Measurements

U.S.	METRIC
1 teaspoon	5 ml
1 tablespoon	15 ml
1/4 cup	60 ml
1/3 cup	75 ml
1/2 cup	125 ml
2/3 cup	150 ml
3/4 cup	175 ml
1 cup	250 ml

Weight Measurements

U.S.	METRIC
1/2 ounce	15 g
1 ounce	30 g
3 ounces	90g
4 ounces	115 g
8 ounces	225 g
12 ounces	350 g
1 pound	450 g
2 1/4 pounds	1 kg

Temperature Conversion

FAHRENHEIT	CELSIUS
250	120
300	150
325	160
350	180
375	190
400	200
425	220
450	230

Almond Butter Oatmeal Puffs 88

Almond Butter Quinoa Bites 125

amaranth 3-4, 22-23, 36, 47, 87

Amaranth and Quinoa Hot Cereal 22

Apple, Almond, and Feta Salad with Honey Chia Dressing 96

Asian Turkey Wraps in Romaine Lettuce 106

Baked Oatmeal 16

Banana Blueberry Muffins 31

barley 3-4, 6, 78-79, 99, 101

Barley Quinoa Pilaf 99

Basic Brown Rice Mix 101

brown rice 2-4, 14, 35-36, 62, 66-67, 73, 78, 80, 87, 100-101, 106, 108-110, 113, 116-117, 126-127

Brown Rice with Herbs, Chicken, and Vegetables 108

buckwheat 4, 14, 35-36, 49

Butternut Squash and Shrimp Pasta 114

Carrot Orange Spice Muffins 34

Cherry Chocolate Chip Oatmeal Cookies 130

chia 5, 90, 96-97

Chicken and Grain Pot Stickers 76

Chocolate Almond Butter Oatmeal 17

Chocolate Chip Cookie Bars 136

Chocolate Zucchini Muffins 41

Cinnanut Oatmeal 18

Citrus Salmon Stir Fry 109

Coconut Brown Rice Pudding with Currants 126

Creamy Spelt Berry Oatmeal 21

Enchiladas 118

flax 5, 16, 21, 62, 90

Garlic Parmesan Baguettes 60

Graham Cracker Bites 89

granola 3, 6, 85, 88, 93, 130

Granola with a Tropical Twist 93

Homemade Hamburgers 50

Indian Flatbread 52

Kamut® 2-3, 5, 14, 21, 28, 31-32, 35-36,

38, 40-41, 47, 50, 60, 62, 80, 87, 113, 124, 129-130, 132-133

lecithin 3, 48, 58

millet 3, 5-6, 25, 101

Millet Cranberry Cereal 25

Nectarine Berry Crumble 133

Oatmeal Cashew Chocolate Chip Cookies 128

Oatmeal Chocolate Chip Cookie Tart 134

Oatmeal Honey Spelt Bread 56

oats 6, 16-19, 21, 47, 80, 84-86, 90-91, 93, 130, 136

Old Fashioned Oatmeal Bars 40

Peach Pie Muffins 32

Pear Ginger Muffins 28

Perfect Whole-Wheat Bread 58

Pesto Pasta with Shrimp 74

pita bread 54-55

pumpkin bread 38-39

quinoa 3, 6-7, 22, 24, 38, 60, 76, 78, 87, 98-99, 101, 125

Quinoa and Teff Hot Cereal 24

Quinoa Fruit Salad 98

Raw Almond Butter Treats 91

Rolled Power Bars 90

Rye 7

Shrimp Salad with Brown Rice 66

spelt 2-3, 7, 11-14, 21, 31-32, 35-36, 38, 40-41, 47, 49-50, 56, 60, 62, 76, 80-81, 87, 89, 113, 122, 129

Spelt Waffles 12

Strawberry Banana Muffins 36

Strawberry Shortcake Bites 122

Strawberry Yogurt Kamut® Cake 124

Sweet and Sour Chicken 116

Sweet and Spicy Barley 78

Sweet Challah Bread 62

Tasty Buttermilk Blueberry Pancakes 15

teff 7, 24, 32, 129

Teriyaki Chicken Berry Salad 73

Tom Kha Gai 110

tortillas 66, 68, 80, 118-119

Turkey and Pesto on Sourdough 72

wheat 2-7, 13, 21, 49-50, 55-56, 58, 60, 75, 132

Whole-Grain Cinnamon Roll Bread 48

Whole-Grain Fruit Bars 86

Whole-Grain Hamburger Buns 50, 104

Whole-Grain Rolls 47

Whole-Grain Tortilla Pizza 68

Whole-Grain Tortillas 68, 80, 118

About Familius

Familius was founded in 2012 with the intent to align the founders' love of publishing and family with the digital publishing renaissance which occurred simultaneously with the Great Recession. The founders believe that the traditional family is the basic unit of society, and that a society is only as strong as the families that create it.

Familius' mission is to help families be happy. We invite you to participate with us in strengthening your family by being part of the Familius family. Go to www.familius. com to subscribe and receive information about our books, articles, and videos.

Website: www.familius.com

Facebook: www.facebook.com/paterfamilius

Twitter: @paterfamilius1 and @familiustalk

Pinterest: www.pinterest.com/familius